The Art *of* Calvados

Christian Drouin

Preface by Jason Wilson

White Mule Press, a division of
American Distilling Institute
PO Box 577
Hayward, CA USA 94541
distilling.com/resources/books

Copyright 2024 © Christian Drouin

All rights reserved.

ISBN 978-1-7369802-9-3

To my wife, Béatrice, for her support in the
ups and downs of this project.

"Calvados is one of the world's great brandies."
— Anthony Dias Blue, *San Jose Mercury News* — Nov 8, 1989

"It's time for the Americans who savor distilled spirits to consider Calvados as a member of their libation repertoire. These are some of the greatest brandies not just from France, but that are available on the world stage at the present time.... I feel that Calvados's place among the brandy greats has yet to be realized, in particular, in the U.S."
— Paul Pacult, *Spirit Journal* — July, 1998

"Calvados: The world's premier apple brandy, one of the best-kept secrets in the world of fine spirit."
— Henrik Mattson, Sweden (2004)

"Calvados: One of the world's great brandies, the finest of apple distillates."
— Michael Jackson, *Bar and Cocktail Book: A Complete Guide to the World's Drinks and How to Mix and Serve Them*, 1995

Introduction:	
The World of Cider Brandy	*3*
Calvados, the Soul of Normandy	*9*
The History of Calvados	*15*
Producing Calvados	*29*
Calvados in Cuisine	*49*
Calvados Recipes	*56*
Calvados at the Bar	*63*
Calvados Cocktails	*74*
Calvados Producers	*89*
Bibliography	*101*

Preface

THERE ARE NO WINE APPELLATIONS in Normandy. Grapes, revered elsewhere in France, are an afterthought in this region that stretches out into the English Channel on France's northwest coast, about a two-hour drive from Paris. The climate is just too unpredictable: hot and sunny one moment, rainy and windy the next.

Forget about grapes in Normandy. Here, the apple is king. Each fall, dozens of apple varieties in field blends, are harvested, crushed and pressed into cider. After resting up to a year, much of that cider in Calvados is distilled into the exquisite apple brandy that takes the region's name.

Outside France, spirits aficionados tend to overlook Calvados when discussing the world's great brandies, with the focus and attention too often on Cognac and Armagnac. But those among us who love the apple brandy from Normandy know what the uninitiated are missing. No less than the great New Yorker writer A.J. Liebling, in his classic food memoir *Between Meals*, declared Calvados "the best alcohol in the world." In Liebling's opinion, Calvados "has a more agreeable bouquet, a warmer touch to the heart, and more outgoing personality than Cognac." Though, he did admit that "not everybody has had the advantage of a good early soaking in the blessed liquid." Thankfully, Christian Drouin did indeed have the advantage of a "good early soaking." Here, he will tell the wonderful story of this "blessed liquid."

Christian's son, Guillaume, once told me: "People who like Calvados like spirits with personality." It's not an overstatement to say that after a meal, Calvados touches the heart warmly. Over the past decade, I've visited Normandy numerous times and Calvados has become one of my favorite spirits. I've also witnessed its continued evolution, one that the Drouin family has a large hand in.

Even within France, Calvados has struggled with its reputation. Sixty years ago, there were about 15,000 Calvados producers in Normandy, most of them unlicensed. These were farmers who distilled apple brandy for personal consumption. Much of it was rough stuff that became known by the slang term *calva* — the sort of thing old men drank with their morning coffee. Now, just over 300 producers remain in the 2,100 square mile region of Calvados, with only about 20 brands that are known outside the region. It has taken time, but slowly, over the past few decades, a serious generation of Calvados producers has elevated the spirit into a conversation with the world's other great brandies.

Still, great Calvados never forgets its rustic roots. Some aspects of tradition are timeless, such as the *trou Normand*, or "the Norman hole," in which Calvados is served between courses at a large meal to cleanse the palate and make room for more. Normandy is still a place of genuine, multi-use farms. There is still a traditional designation of fermier ("farm-made") Calvados. You'll see hand-made signs for it as you drive along the Route du Cidre, a 25-mile loop that winds through orchards and picturesque villages of half-timbered houses like Bonnebosq, Beaufour-Druval, Beuvron-en-Auge, and Cambremer. If you stop at a sign that reads "Cru de Cambremer," the farm probably has a small tasting room where you can try their cider, brandy and pommeau de Normandie, a blend of Calvados and fresh-pressed juice.

Pays d'Auge consists of 3,252 hectares, with 59 producers in total, though only around 15 or so are widely known in export markets. It is the most prestigious of Calvados' three appellations, and is also where some of France's most famed cheeses are made in the towns of Camembert, Pont-l'Évêque, and Livarot. Many Calvados producers here are also dairy farmers. The best orchard sites may also be where herds of cows graze throughout summer under the apple trees. This is the case even in the orchards of top producers.

There's true synergy in this shared agriculture. As the fruit ripens on the trees, the cows grazing in the orchard start getting hungry for apples, and begin thumping the trunks to make them fall. When the first apples do fall, the cows devour them off the ground. "The cows are doing our job for us," I was told by the Drouin family. "Because the first apples they make fall are overripe or diseased or somehow unusable. And once we see them begin to eat those apples, we move the cows from the orchard. That's when I know it's about time for harvest."

Making quality cider and brandy begins in the orchard, to rework the old wine cliché. The blend of varieties is critical. Apples for cider, and Calvados, are very different than the shiny Gala, Jonagold, or Honeycrisp you buy at the supermarket. There are dozens of varieties that producers can use, categorized as sweet, sharp, bittersweet and bittersharp.

Bittersweet and bittersharp are the most important, and they're often gnarled and tiny, the size of deformed golf balls and so tart and tannic that you'd spit out the first bite. Calvados requires a high percentage of bittersharp and bittersweet apple varieties with names like Antoinette, Frequin Rouge, Bisquet, Moulin à Vent, or Mettais. These bring the acidity and tannins necessary for structure and long aging. They're blended with a smaller percentage of sweet varieties like Rouge Duret or Noël des Champs along with sharps, or acidic apples, like Rambaud, Petit Jaune, or René Martin. A major reason why most American apple brandy has nowhere near the complexity of Calvados is because it's mostly made with culinary or dessert apples rather than tannic, sharp cider varieties.

Once the apples are crushed and pressed, cider is made. "You can't make good Calvados if you don't make good cider," Drouin says. For the best producers, cider fermentation is natural and slow. Traditionally, cider can rest for up to a year in old barrels before it's distilled, usually just before the new harvest.

Outside of Pays d'Auge, many producers include a small amount of pears in their younger Calvados. Pears are higher in acidity and often create a softer, delicate spirit. In the unique blends from Domfrontais AOC, pears become even more significant. The Domfrontais just achieved AOC status in 1997. Before that, most of the Calvados here was clandestine and illegal. There is a famous story about the creation of Comte Louis de Lauriston. The "Comte" on the label is not just a name; in 1962, the actual count was asked to arbitrate an aggressive resistance against the excise tax collectors by locals who surrounded the government officials with tractors and farm tools. The count agreed to maintain a cellar under which the producers could store and market their Calvados legally, as the cooperative Chais du Verger Normand. The brand is now produced and sold by Christian Drouin.

After the orchard, pressing, fermentation, and distillation comes the most important aspect of producing Calvados: aging. This is where house styles truly come into play. There are very few rules on barrel aging in Calvados, and the range of techniques and approaches is wide. Sometimes, there are experiments with oak finishes, such as Christian Drouin's finishes in Sauternes, Port, or Banyuls casks. Regardless of approach, many believe the greatest Calvados come from 30 or more years in the barrel. To be clear, quality in Calvados is not simply a question of long aging. There is good Calvados at every age, even just a few years old. In fact, young Calvados is much more drinkable and enjoyable than young Cognac or Armagnac.

Vintages in Calvados can also be tricky. First of all, vintage is a bit of a misnomer when talking about apples instead of grapes. Next, a vintage in Calvados only means something if you know when the spirit was bottled (and thus its age). Finally, you need to know what "vintage" means to a particular producer. Christian Drouin, for instance, offers a deep roster of vintages, and for them, a vintage is the year the cider is distilled — meaning the year after the apples were harvested. That said, most producers offer a vintage because they feel a particular brandy offers something special, and so these bottles will always be at a premium.

What are we looking for when we taste great Calvados? Guillaume Drouin once told me that great Calvados should have ambition. "This is more complex than even a premier cru of Bordeaux or Burgundy," he told me while tasting Christian Drouin's 1963 vintage. Others will tell you they believe Calvados should always maintain a core (no pun intended) of beautiful rusticity. One critical aspect, for many enthusiasts, is that there should always be some note, however fleeting or haunting, of the actual apple from the orchard.

In younger Calvados, that might come across as ripe, crisp fruit or perhaps apple pie or strudel. But in older Calvados, the unmistakable aromas and savory, astringent notes of the apple's peel is an indicator of quality. In this way Calvados is quite different from grape brandies like Cognac and Armagnac. Paul Cezanne once famously declared, "With an apple, I will astonish Paris!" With that apple transformed into Calvados, it shall be more than just Parisians who will be astonished

— *by Jason Wilson*

Introduction: The World of Cider Brandy

THE ORIGINAL APPLE from which all those we know today descend was found in Kazakhstan, and more specifically in the Almaty area at the foot of the Tian massif. I went there once and had a bite of one of those produced nowadays with great emotion: beautiful, big, delicious apples, said to resist illnesses and insect bites with no need of any chemical treatment.

Baptized M*alus sieversii*, these apples spread through commercial routes wherever the climate was favorable. Thanks to chance and human intervention, varieties have multiplied infinitely during their migrations. The Romans contributed to their expansion throughout Europe and up to Britain. Then, from Normandy and Britain, the apple swept across North America, where its arrival dates back to the early 17th century.

For a very long time, people have used what nature offered them to produce alcoholic drinks. Fermented cider and cider spirits are produced pretty much everywhere around the world. I have tasted some in Kazakhstan, Japan, Russia, Sweden, Italy, Germany, Argentina, Canada, and in the United States, but spirits made from table apples never match the complexity of Norman Calvados produced from cider apples.

When it comes to apple brandy, the first country you think of might be France with its famed Calvados, but Spain, Great Britain and the United States also have their traditions. Cider production stemming from cider apples is as old in Spain as it is in Normandy, where only its hygienic qualities were appreciated before the 16th century. Thanks to apple varieties imported from Biscay to northwestern Spain, it then became appreciated also for its tasting quality. These varieties were imported to Cotentin by gentlemen agronomists. Combined with local varieties, they made possible a unique orchard inventory that was the basis for exceptional cider spirit production.

I went to Northwestern Spain in the early 1980's and tasted good quality spirits. At that time the area was facing a shortage of fruits, and Norman cider apples were sent to San Sebastian to enable the Basques to keep drinking cider. The traditional orchards had been neglected for many years. Low-stem (dwarf) orchards were being planted on soils allowing easier maintenance but, to my mind, were less qualified for quality production of cider or brandy. I haven't had the opportunity to taste any since then.

In England, cider distilling died out a long time ago. Distillation of cider into brandy was popular in the U.K. until cheap gin began to be shipped from the Netherlands around 1700 after William of Orange accessed the throne. The last official record of cider distilling in the U.K. occurred during the reign of Queen Anne in the early 18th century. Then, in October 1984, operating with a museum license, Bulmer Ltd., the largest British cidery, started production of cider brandy under the name of King Offa's distillery.

King Offa's has since closed, but Julian Temperley, who makes award-winning cider in Somerset, together with Charles Clive-Ponsonby, a Somerset landowner, decided to revive this ancient art in 1987. Their objective was to produce a version of Calvados from local cider. Temperley set off to France to buy a second-hand column still found by William Leyshon, an English thatcher living in Normandy. Cider was produced from local cider apples, distilled and aged in second-hand sherry casks. After a long struggle with Customs and Excise he was granted the First U.K. Excise license by HM Customs, and the first bottles of Somerset Royal Cider Brandy were released in 1991. Cider Brandy, once an illicit liquor, is now legally produced in Somerset.

I began following this adventure on January 5th, 1988, when I received a letter from Temperley congratulating me for my book *Le Grand Livre du Calvados*, which had been published in 1987. He told me he was planning to visit Normandy and would very much like to meet me and visit our artisanal distillery. Temperley and his wife visited us a few months later. We were both at the start of an adventure and it was a very interesting opportunity to share.

On October 12, 1988, he wrote to me that "your visit to Japan may have been the cause of an inquiry we have had today. A London firm of buying agents phoned for a price for 18 000 liters of juice to be shipped to Japan" for trial production of apple brandy. Indeed, Japan produces apple brandy from local apples as well as from imported apple juice or cider spirits.

The Temperly's at Somerset Cider Brandy Co.

We communicated again when Temperley had to face another challenge: Brussels regulated spirits produced from cider or perry as "cider spirits" and "perry spirits." In the United States, they are named apple brandy. Temperley had named his product "Somerset Cider Brandy."

Then, Spanish brandy makers complained to the European Union that the term "brandy" should be used only for spirits distilled from grapes. The Spanish authorities warned Temperley that, unless he could prove the term "Cider Brandy" was in use in the country before a regulation defining all European spirits was drawn up six years earlier, he could be ruled out of order. Then the Scotch Whisky Association backed Spain! A miserable treachery!

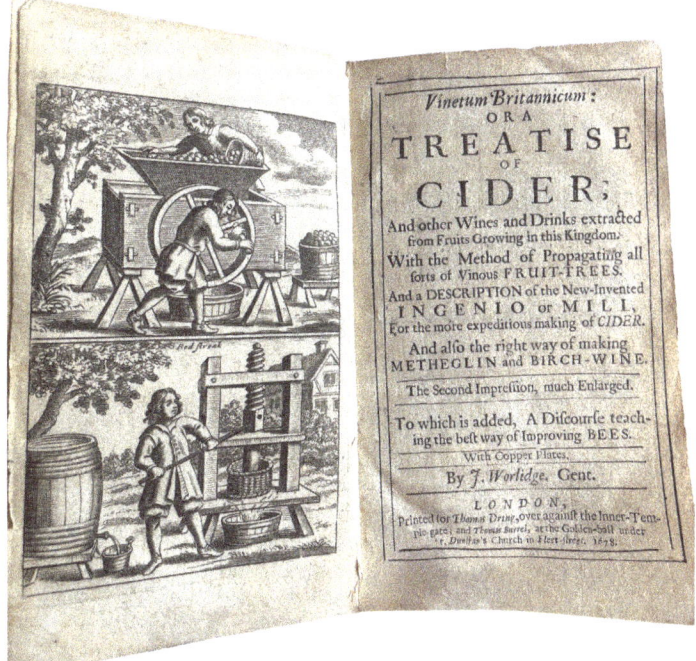

The claim could have put him out of business by forcing him to change the name of his Somerset Cider Brandy. It was a long battle, but Temperley succeeded in proving that the term "cider brandy" derived from an historic tradition of apple brandy manufacturing in Britain, backed by a reference he found in a book written in 1678.

On September 23, 2011, Temperley wrote to me: "After four years and a lot of problems, mainly from the Spanish, helped by Scots, we were last week granted a PGI (Protected Geographical Indication), and the name Somerset Cider Brandy was added to Annex three of EU Council Regulation 110/2008. The use of the term Cider Brandy is not allowed in EU/UK law except for Somerset Cider Brandy. Very strict product specifications are published by The Department for Environment, Food & Rural affairs." While writing this book, I tasted a 20-year-old bottle of Somerset Cider Brandy given to me by Matilda Temperley, his daughter, now managing director of the Somerset Cider Brandy company. I must confess the product is very good, a most respectable cousin to AOC Calvados, reminding us that for a period of time, Normandy and Britain were ruled by the same kings.

During my first trip to New York, a long time ago, I was interested in knowing what American cider tasted like. It was in October, and along Central Park I found a market where farmers were selling cider by the glass. I was quite surprised at discovering I was tasting plain apple juice. I had no idea that in the United States "cider" referred to apple juice, while the fermented beverage from apple juice was called "hard cider".

In colonial America, fermenting juice was a way to make it last, and hard cider was as common as beer. Apple brandy made by distilling hard cider is most likely the first spirit produced from local agriculture in North America. Stills were known to be in the U.S. as early as 1683. Freezing fermented apple cider to concentrate its alcohol was a common "distilling" method for farmers who did not own stills. Apple brandy has been part of American history since the 18th century, and came into existence a century before bourbon, which was a cheaper alternative.

"Applejack" and "apple brandy" are often used interchangeably to refer to a spirit made from apples, but there are important differences. Lisa Laird Dunn, president of Laird & Company in New Jersey, helped me to clarify the distinction between the two: "The Laird family assisted in the creation of the blended applejack standard of identity.

The reason being the consumer taste profile in the late 1960's moved from straight aged brown spirits. The blended applejack category allowed us to lighten the spirit to align with the consumers' palate. I agree that blending the product with neutral spirits did in fact lower the cost, but it was not the primary reason. The ability to produce this lighter, blended spirit kept my family's company viable and allowed us to preserve the historic apple brandies as well."

Applejack may be 100% apple brandy, or it may be a combination of apple and neutral spirits. A spirit labeled blended applejack may contain up to 80% neutral spirits blended with a minimum of 20% apple brandy and aged for at least two years, whereas apple brandy has to be 100% distilled apple spirit.

Sadly, these original American spirituous beverages, apple brandy and hard cider, collapsed under the blows of the temperance movement culminating in the prohibition of alcohol (1920-1933). To prevent the production of hard cider and apple brandy, orchards and stills were destroyed. Most of the knowhow acquired in the production of apple brandy disappeared. Not until the end of the 20th century did one witness the renaissance of apple brandy in North America, when it was reborn due to the phenomenal success of craft cocktail culture and the resulting renewed interest of bartenders in forgotten character and quality products.

Laird & Company, established in 1780, is the oldest distillery in the United States. The New Jersey company claims "to produce the vast majority of all applejack and American apple brandy on the market, which has been enjoyed since colonial times." Not only has Laird been the leading domestic producer of apple brandy and applejack blended brandy, but for many years, it was the *only* domestic producer. During Prohibition the family kept the company in operation by producing non-alcoholic apple products until 1933, when Laird & Co was granted a federal license to produce apple brandy for "medicinal purposes." In the early 1940's the Laird family acquired the current distillery in Virginia. With the disappearance of farmland in New Jersey, the entire production is now distilled in Virginia using only fresh Virginia apples. In a high end New York bar, I was given the opportunity to taste some aged apple brandies from Laird that I really enjoyed.

Joseph T. Laird in Scobeyville, NJ.

The apple brandy category has recently grown from a one-house category to a livelier one after the entrance of a bunch of craft producers that make Laird's less lonely. All over the country, new players have joined Laird's in the domestic brandy category.

Without longstanding traditions to guide them, and without strictly regulated AOC requirements like Calvados, American apple brandy doesn't play by a strict set of rules. The lax definition fails to establish a baseline of category-wide standards, which gives modern distillers great freedom to experiment and create their products. Given the diversity of American soils and climate and the diversity of apple varieties available, distillers today offer a very large range of products under the category of "apple brandy."

American producers can choose to ferment by wild yeast, or by introducing a cultured yeast. They have a choice of stainless steel or copper stills, single or double distillation, and whether or not to age their products — and, if so, for how long. They also have their choice of barrels: new or old, American or European oak, and various char and toast levels. They have, in other words, unlimited opportunities to create their own apple brandy. Some distillers strive to go back to time-honored colonial methods, others seek to unlock the secret of Calvados going so far as to import apple varieties from Normandy, and others look for their own way to create new traditions. This situation results in a variety of products whose character and quality vary considerably from one to another. In such conditions, do the new players constitute a true American apple brandy category?

The majority of them are also producers of whiskey, wine, or other spirits who added apple spirits to their portfolio when bartenders created a trend for forgotten products. Clear Creek Distillery in Oregon is a kind of exception, as they started producing unaged Oregon pear brandy, as well as aged apple brandies matured in new French Limousin oak, in 1985. I remember tasting very pure products from this company. Vermont is the home of a great number of apple orchards. According to Sean Ludford, to my mind one of the best connoisseurs of Calvados in America, Vermont Spirits Distilling co. produces a great American take on Calvados. Other names on the market include Shady Knoll Apple Brandy, a family-owned and operated farm and craft distillery in the Hudson River Valley of New York; Finger Lakes Distilling Co., a farm distillery in New York State; Baltimore Spirits Co. claiming to produce new world spirits through old world distillation; Catoctin Creek Distilling in Virginia; Copper & Kings American Brandy Co. in Louisville, Kentucky; Wollersheim Apple Brandy distilled from Wisconsin apples and aged in Wisconsin oak barrels; Huber's Starlight Distillery, established in 2001 by Greg and Ted Huber to distill spirits in Indiana, a short drive from Louisville, Kentucky; Santa Fe Spirits Apple Brandy in northern New Mexico founded by Colin Keegan in 2010; Sonoma Cider Apple Brandy in Sonoma Valley; and St. George Spirits in Alameda, California.

Consumers are nowadays willing to try new experiences, explore craft food and drinks, and learn how they are made. We are witnessing a new resurgence of interest in apple cider and apple brandies. According to an October 2023 report from Verified Market Reports, the global apple brandy market is anticipated to grow at a steady rate in the coming years. Apples are grown in a wide variety of locations across the country and apple brandy is well-suited to the needs of craft distillers. However, the category still has a way to go before it is widely understood and appreciated by consumers. Compounding the lack of education and awareness is the fact that apple brandy is more expensive to produce than grain whiskey. There is a lot of educational work to be done. In my opinion, this can be achieved if producers around the world cooperate to create a strong apple category able to compete with the other spirits categories.

My original project was to produce a book which would be published under the title "the world of cider brandies." I suggested to Mathilda Temperley and Lisa Laird Dunn that the three of us could work together on this publication. Both showed interest. In a mail dated May 28, 2020, Lisa Laird Dunn wrote to me "It is wonderful to hear from you and thank you for thinking of the Laird family for this project. I wholeheartedly agree with your assessment regarding the quality of cider brandy and how underrated they are as a category. I would be happy to further discuss how we can take part to champion the education of our storied brandies." But such a project would require a lot of workand still has to be implemented..

Calvados, the Soul of Normandy

THE SMALL, HIGHLY AROMATIC CIDER APPLE is the fruit of sun, rain, and wind, a fruit that is the very soul of Normandy: yellow, red, green, russet, with a smooth skin and white flesh. It bears pretty French names — such as petit jaune, argile grise, argile rouge, frequin rouge, binet rouge, rouge duret, joly rouge, rouge mulot, rouge folie, pomme de cheval, pomme de Rouen, doux-évêque, belle-cauchoise, cuisse-madame, and many others.

Cider is a beverage born from the slow fermentation of cider apple juice during the winter. It is a healthy, joyful drink: sweet, semi-dry, dry. From cider comes Calvados — the quintessence of the apple. It delights both soul and palate. It is perhaps the finest eau-de-vie in the world.

If you have doubts, pour yourself an old Calvados into a tulip-shaped wine glass, preferably made of crystal. Turn it slowly so it coats the sides of the glass, admire it, and then warm it slowly, slightly, in the palm of your hand; hold it up, but not too close, to your nose, and take the time to fall under its spell.

Calvados long remained a secret. It is now found in most major cities. The name resonates in all four corners of the world like a standard-bearer of the Norman flag. It draws tribute in various languages from journalists, critics, and sommeliers. It is the subject of books. Starred chefs and mixologists place it at the heart of their art.

For Calvados to have become a product recognized by all lovers of venerable eaux-de-vie, it took know-how and telling, distilling cider and distilling words. The know-how is age-old. It is both a science and an art.

The history that transformed wild apples from the ancient forests of Normandy into the Calvados we now know spans centuries. It was necessary to identify the soils, select the varieties, and improve them through successive grafting. It was necessary to care for the apple trees, to prune them, to establish subtle combinations of bitter, bittersweet, sweet, tart, sour, early, mid-season, late. And it was necessary to harvest them by shaking and beating the tree, gathering the apples, mashing, crushing, grating, squeezing the pulp to extract the juice and then placing it in tanks, barreling it, racking it. in tanks, barrel, rack.

Once fermentation is over, the must that has turned into cider enters the mysterious world of stills and retorts. The distiller, heir to the alchemists, exposes the cider to flames in pot stills in the Pays d'Auge area, or to column stills in the Domfrontais area. He then cuts the heads and the tails to keep only the heart, the "coeur de chauffe," a colorless, ardent, scented eau-de-vie, *la blanche*, destined to spend a long time in oak casks. There are many types of cask: Normandy oak, Limousin oak, Hungarian oak, new wood from which the sap has been removed, and wood used to age Port, sherry or Madeira wines. With the discrete complicity of the wood, air, and time, the eau-de-vie acquires color, bouquet, and body: it becomes yellow, gold, orange, topaz, amber, and mahogany. It evolves to become weak or strong, refined, distinguished, with ordinary or coarse smells of fresh fruit transforming into apple, pear, dry fruit, flowers, and spices. And then the work continues. It is still necessary to to top barrels, to blend or select vintages, to filter, to bottle, to ship, and to pay various levies before drinking. The result? Sélection, vieux, VSOP, XO, hors d'âge, âge inconnu, long drink, short drink, flambage, déglaçage, à la Normande, Vallée d'Auge, Trou Normand, sorbet, granité, digestif. Calvados makes for good digestion just as it fires the senses.

Long confined to its area of production in northern France owing to an iniquitous decree of King Louis XIV, Normandy cider apples have resumed their glorious march. Strengthened by their know-how, modern distillers have turned into communicators. They talk about Normandy eau-de-vie as though it were a beautiful woman, admiring her robe, legs, brilliance, scent, an eau-de-vie you kiss squarely on the mouth in an endless embrace! An eau-de-vie that monopolizes our senses.

Calvados, great lord of a hedonistic culture, holds out the promise of voluptuousness.

Calvados, the world's premier apple brandy, was born in Normandy, and is the product of its soil, climate, inhabitants' work and history.

▶ **Normandy**

Normandy was formed by Norsemen, otherwise known as Vikings. Scandinavian seafaring pirates and traders invaded both sides of the Seine River, as well as the nearby northwestern coast of France, in the 9th century. The first Viking leader to rule Normandy under the name of Count of Rouen was Rollo. A treaty signed by French King Charles Le Simple and Rollo in 911 is considered the founding of Normandy. In 1066 at the battle of Hastings, Rollo's descendant William the Conqueror conquered England, which was ruled by Normans until the mid-13th century.

More powerful than the Kingdom of France during the Middle Ages, the ancient Duchy of Normandy has remained a most striking region. Its wealth and glory mainly come from the versatility of its landscapes, mingling the pale blue of the sky with the haze of white clouds, the beige of large sandy beaches, the white of steep chalky cliffs, and the multiple shades of its fields and meadows where cows and horses graze in the shade of orchards.

The quality of the soil combined with the influence of humid, damp, and changable weather explains why cattle and horse breeding and apple orchards are on equal footing in Normandy. The rich, thick, green grass of Pays d'Auge and Manche where Normand cows pasture enables them to produce some of the best milk and dairy products France has to offer. There is nothing like fresh Norman butter or ivory-colored thick, velvety double cream. The same cow milk is used to produce Norman cheese, among which four have an Appellation d'Origine Protégée (AOP): Neufchâtel, produced in Pays de Bray, in the North of Normandy; Camembert de Normandie, the world-famous Norman cheese; and Pont-L'Evêque and Livarot produced in the heart of Pays d'Auge.

Around 115,000 horses are bred in Normandy annually. It is home to Le Haras National du Pin, which was created by King Louis XIV and is famous for being the "Château de Versailles" of horses, as well as the Pôle International du Cheval in Deauville, a temple of equestrian sports. Deauville-Normandy Airport's growing traffic is partially due to horses – and their owners – traveling back and forth from one country to another. Indeed, most French champions are raised in Pays d'Auge on stud estates, and their owners come from all over the world to spend time during the summer on racing fields, the most famous of all being Deauville. They also play or watch polo games, walk and sunbathe on lovely sandy beaches, play golf,, smash balls on Norman tennis courts, and admire the most gorgeous sunsets while sipping a cocktail or having dinner on the seashore.

Mobile iron still known as the "pivet hot water bottle", manufactured in 1946 to the plans of Pierre Pivet

There is one constant all around Normandy: its orchards of apple trees, almost all composed of cider apple trees of many different varieties. There are also large, majestic pear trees, often one or two centuries old, mostly set in the Domfromtais area, around the lovely middle-aged city of Domfront.

Famous Norman apple and pear cider are made from the juice of these bitter, bittersweet, sour, or sweet apples, which are not good for eating but savory and full of flavor as a sparkling drink. Similarly, pear cider can be made from the juice of small, tart pears that are quite different from William (Bartlett) pears. Cider and "poiré" (perry) are used not only to pair with food, but also as a cooking ingredient to help add flavor to delicious creamy sauces that are typical in Norman cuisine. They are also increasingly used to top cocktails. Alongside with Camembert cheese and cider, Calvados, a centuries old cider spirit, is one of the symbols of Normandy that has reached consumers all around the world

▶ The Challenges of a Farm-Scale Enterprise

My Calvados story begins in the early '60s when my father, Christian Drouin Sr. bought a farm on the hills of Gonneville sur Honfleur called "Les Fiefs Sainte Anne." The estate was covered in apple trees. Like many farmers, he could have sold the apples to a local cidery, but after realizing the area was famous for the exceptional qualities of its Calvados, he was soon driven by the desire to produce his own spirit. If he was going to produce Calvados, it had to be one of the very best.

My father decided to first build a significant stock of high-quality Calvados from which he would later start a small business. With the help of two passionate artisans, Pierre Pivet, a third-generation artisan distiller named by *Deauville Passion* magazine the "Mozart of the still;" and Marius Duchemin, a fifth-generation cooper in Honfleur, he spent twenty years developing stock, adhering to time honored methods of distilling and aging Calvados. The Calvados casks, including former Port and sherry casks, were stored in the old half-timbered, thatch-roofed buildings of the farm. He also acquired several batches of very old Calvados when the estates of some well-reputed producers were sold. In 1971, his Calvados — still in barrel — won its first awards in regional competitions and in Paris.

Our family used to spend most weekends on the farm, and I enjoyed every season: spring with the spectacular apple trees blossoming while Pierre Pivet used his mobile still in the farm courtyard, producing appley aromas; summer with its powerful fragrance floating above the trees; fall with all the small apples of all colors hanging heavy on the trees, and heaps of apples ripening on the floor until the mobile press came and started its work of juice extraction; and even winter, with rustic leafless apple trees standing against the sky. At that time, I was not yet thinking of becoming a Calvados producer, though I was my father's enthusiastic supporter.

In 1969, my father offered me the chance to become a partner in the company he was creating, SNC Drouin et Cie. I was pleased with the proposal and invested all my pocket money into the company. At the time, I was studying political science and law, and was not thinking of running the show. It was only ten years later, in 1979, that stocks of well-aged Calvados were considered sufficient enough to allow sales to begin. Each barn of the estate was full of barrels, and my father was too busy to start the business. He talked me into coming back from Canada, where I was enjoying a great life with my wife and my two young children Florence and Guillaume, to join him. Guillaume, a few months old at that time, was to join the company at the end of 2003 and is now our CEO.

When I started working in the business, my goal was to start one of the best cellars for Calvados Pays d'Auge and to earn international recognition. Turning my back to the culture of café-calva, a rustic mixture of Calvados and coffee, in a sector still highly regionalized and dominated by sales of young Calvados, I had in mind a quite different future for this spirit. I was fascinated by the art of aging and, thanks to the stocks my father had accumulated, I specialized in the production of the rarest and oldest Calvados.

Having spent almost ten years abroad in Iran and Canada and traveled in many countries, I naturally decided to give the business an international orientation. Our first export markets in the early to mid 1980s were Canada, Belgium, Germany, and the U.K., followed by the United States, Japan, Hong Kong, and Singapore in 1986. I found that niche products like Calvados are not well known outside their country of origin. While meeting professionals and consumers in France and all over the world, I answered many questions about Calvados production, history, and consumption, which indicated to me a lack of knowledge of Calvados, but also a steadily growing interest and desire to learn more about the spirit.

As I looked for books to recommend, I realized there was no book published about Calvados and decided to write the first one with a friend of mine, Jacques Billy. The book, called *Le Grand Livre des Calvados* was published in France in 1987.

Since the book was published, the Calvados and cocktail world has greatly changed, and it was the right time for an updated publication. In 2020, I published a new book in French, *Le Livre des Calvados*, and one in Japanese, *Calvados Book*. But I wanted to share my 45 years of experience with more readers by publishing a book in English, as more than 60 percent of all Calvados production is now exported.

FABRICATION DU CIDRE — 5. La Pression du marc

I hope it will give a proper answer to all those who ask: What is Calvados? How should I enjoy it? These are questions producers would rather not have to answer, but that I have heard so often when traveling all over the United States. In the '80s and '90s, Calvados in the U.S. was mostly perceived as a cooking ingredient. The bottles that one could find on liquor store shelves were not the kind that could induce enthusiasm from fine spirits connoisseurs. In those days it was difficult to find high-end Calvados, which was a concern for finer restaurants and liquor stores.

In the early '80s, Peter Morell, one of the most famous wine and spirit merchants in New York City, tasted our 25-year-old Calvados at Vinexpo Bordeaux and became our first customer in the U.S., although I did not have an importer yet. Both my first agents, Stanley Stankiwicz and Frederick Seggerman, did a splendid job making Calvados better known, organizing tastings and introducing me to spirits experts. I still remember Stanley Stankiwicz taking me to Anthony Dias Blue's home in San Francisco; he loved the 25-year-old Calvados. As for Fred Seggerman, he organized an unlikely meeting in the back of a small pizzeria in mid-Manhattan with spirits critic

Paul Pacult in 1994. We tasted many vintages out of small plastic cups, and Paul wrote a lot of notes and concluded that Calvados was an awfully underrated category. With Fred Seggerman, I also met Sean Ludford who at that time was the buyer of Sam's in Chicago. Having fallen in love with Calvados, he filled the shelves with an incredible assortment of products.

In addition to explaining how Calvados is produced and how to enjoy it, I would like to develop subjects that might be of interest to Americans such as the role of Calvados in the Battle of Normandy in 1944. I also intend to develop Calvados as a base for cocktails, as it is still considered by most people to be a digestive or cooking ingredient, but is now riding the wave of new trends, especially in cocktails.

369. - Environs de LOUVIERS (Eure). - LES PLANCHES. - Le bouilleur de cru.

FABRICATION DU CIDRE
3. Le Broyage des Pommes à la Meule

The History of Calvados

NOBODY KNOWS EXACTLY WHEN Norman farmers started distilling cider. From the earliest times, wild apple trees have grown in Normandy. Two thousand years ago, the Roman conquerors reported encountering great numbers of them.

Disciplined planting, cultivation, pruning, and grafting of apple trees, however, began in the 8th century, when Charlemagne established the first rules for making cider. The Museum of Normandy in Caen owns the earthenware head of a still discovered during an excavation in Lisieux, in Pays d'Auge, which is believed to be from the 13th century. Though this discovery proves that people distilled in the Middle Ages in Normandy, there is no evidence that the stills were used to distill cider spirit.

Not before the 16th century, however, did distilled spirits become a regular drink. Until then, they were only used for medicine. This was attested when Jean Liebault (1535-1596), a French medical doctor, wrote about the medical virtues of cider and perry spirit. However, in 1606, a closed guild of apple brandy distillers called the Brotherhood of Cider Spirit Distillers of Normandy was formed, and a job that had belonged to the apothecaries became that of the distillers

Gilles de Gouberville, a Norman country nobleman, is said in many publications to have distilled the first cider spirit in 1553. However, the only thing one learns in his manuscript is that Gilles de Gouberville had a still made to distill "his waters," without any information on which waters were distilled. Although the distillation of cider seems likely, nothing proves it.

In the 16th century, Norman farmers began experimenting with grafting Spanish cider apples on Norman apple trees, creating new varieties that significantly improved the quality of cider they produced, changing the status of Norman cider from hygienic beverage (water from wells and ponds was unsafe) to enjoyable drink. Then, thanks to the progress made in distillation, Cider spirit produced in Normandy became a fearsome rival to the wine spirits produced in the south of France at the beginning of the 18th century. The improvement of cider spirit, and even its superiority to products from the

Gironde or Aunis areas, enabled it to conquer export markets in Northern Europe. Such success unleashed true tempests against the Norman spirit.

In 1713, France's southern regions rose up and obtained an edict from aging King Louis XIV forbidding cider spirit to be exported, not only abroad but also to other parts of the French realm. In its preamble the edict declared that this was "meant to favor turnover of wine spirits." In admonitions to the King, the Parliament of Normandy considered the edict as being iniquitous. Had it not existed, Calvados would now be likely to have the position that was unfairly gained by Cognac. The edict was abolished soon after the 1789 French Revolution. However, distribution networks had vanished and it was not until the end of the 20th century that Calvados found its way to export markets again.

The grape phylloxera crisis of the late 19th century destroyed a large part of French vineyards and deprived consumers of wine and Cognac, yet it opened a golden era for cider and Calvados. Apple trees were massively planted, and soon Normandy countryside was covered with apple orchards. First limited to Normandy, Calvados was progressively consumed all over France thanks to the rural exodus that led Norman farmers to the suburbs of industrial cities. During the First World War, Norman soldiers helped those from other French regions discover the Norman apple brandy. This was when Calvados began its transformation from the drink of farmers and workers, to the base of cocktails created by legendary bartenders in palatial hotel bars.

In the second half of the 19th century, Norman cider brandy increasingly began to be marketed under the name Calvados. People often ask me where the name Calvados comes from. The origin of the name is still an enigma. After the French revolution in 1790, the Province of Normandy was replaced by five new administrative districts and the name Calvados was given to the one surrounding Caen, after two bare rocky points along the coast named Calvados. The name Calvados was given to the cider spirit produced in the region from the 19th century onward. In 1942, it became an official appellation.

But where did those rocky points get their name? A legend says that a ship from the Spanish Invincible Armada named El Calvador or San Salvador, while on her way to invade England, faced a huge storm and foundered off the Norman coast on two bare rocky points in 1588. It gave them its name, which ultimately became Calvados. But no record of the shipwreck was ever found. I personally visited the Maritime Museum in Greenwich near London and was unable to find a ship named El Calvador in a book giving the list of Spanish ships. I found a ship named San Salvador, but she never wrecked along the Norman coast. Another explanation given by René Lepelley, Professor at the University of Caen, says the word Calvador found on an old marine map from 1653 would have a Latin origin, "cava dorsa," which means something like "bare coast."

▶ Calvados and World War II

World War II was of decisive importance for Calvados, giving it, if not an enhanced image, at least international notoriety. Even before the war broke out, many Jews, communists, and opponents to the Nazi régime from Germany and Eastern Europe took refuge in France, where they discovered Calvados in Paris bistros. The famous German writer Erich Maria Remarque is partially to thank for the knowledge of Calvados spreading across the world. In his 1945 novel *Arch of Triumph*, action takes place in refugee circles during the winter of 1938-1939; the hero, Ravic, a German surgeon who fled to Paris, sought peace of mind in the spirits served on Paris bistro counters, and in particular, in Calvados, which flows endlessly from beginning to end of the novel. Countless times in the United States, Russia, Ukraine, or Japan, people have referred to this novel as soon as I talk to them about Calvados.

Most of these refugees were handed over to the Nazis by the French Vichy authorities and perished in concentration camps without trace. A few managed to leave France thanks to their contacts. Arthur Koestler, a Hungarian Jew and former communist militant who became a major 20th century author, successfully reached London. When he returned to France after Liberation, he reminisced about the virtues of Calvados, as in an anecdote described in the book co-written by Arthur and Cynthia Koestler called *Stranger on the Square* (Hutchinson 1984). Cynthia, his secretary, who much later became his wife, describes how one day in 1948, to her great surprise, Arthur asked her to stay for dinner. He was expecting friends: the English publisher Hamish Hamilton, his wife and their son:

"We sat down to an orgiastic meal at the candlelit dining table. Soup, followed by fish and entrée, were brought in...White and red wine were in abundance... The guests were enjoying the kind of food and wine which could not be had in England, where food rationing was even more severe than during the war. After the meat course they began to feel that they could take no more and apologetically explained to their host that they were no longer in training after living in puritan England. At this point Arthur said he would give them something which would miraculously dispel the feeling of overeating; it would burn a passage into their gullets and they would be able to enjoy the rest of the meal. He paused dramatically. It was called, he said, a "Trou Normand." He then produced four little glasses and filled them up with Calvados. He urged everybody to follow his example and swallow the drink in one gulp."

The international renown of Calvados owes a lot to these writers and others, like George Simenon, who had Inspector Maigret observe the rite of coffee-calva, a simple mixture of Calvados and coffee, at bistro counters.

Calvados is closely bound up with the darkest hours in French history. The horrifying martyrdom of Normandy clearly saved the rest of France, and Calvados always lay at the heart of events. During World War II, Normandy was first occupied by the Germans and then liberated by the Allies, which enabled Calvados to be discovered by people of all nationalities taking part into the conflict.

With the arrival of German troops in Normandy, distillers tried to hide their stills, as the occupiers were on the lookout for copper to make weapons. Others were prepared to sell their Calvados to the occupiers, or later to the allies. Some of the occupying troops had no compunctions about helping themselves, and happily looted the cellars. Even the French state requisitioned the available alcohol. As a result, a large number of distillers tried to hide their Calvados reserves.

The minister of agriculture at the time, Leroy Ladurie, who hailed from Normandy, worried about the stock of Calvados—which, unlike Cognac, was not protected by

an appellation and could therefore be requisitioned by the State to supply the army and make ammunition. To protect Calvados and eau-de-vie de cidre stocks from being requisitioned by the French government and German occupying forces, he gave apple brandies Appellation d'Origine Contrôlée (AOC) and Appellation d'Origine Réglementée (AOR) status in 1942.

None of these measures managed to save the stock of old Calvados, which disappeared with the plundering of both the occupying forces and the liberators, the bombardments, and, finally, the devastating Battle of Normandy. The cellars of many châteaux were looted. Some of the châtelains" whose estate was requisitioned by German, and then by American, officers occasionally managed to hide their most valuable bottles. Count Louis de Lauriston showed me a few eau-de-vie de cidre bottles distilled in the 19th century that his family had successfully hidden under the rafters of one of his castle towers and which had escaped Marshal Rommel and the American generals' notice.

The Occupation did not, however, prevent peasants from continuing to distill their cider throughout that period. Since distillation never truly ceased, Allied soldiers then in turn discovered Norman apple brandy after the landing. As the stocks of aged Calvados had vanished, the freshly distilled, un-watered available spirit was quite sharp. American soldiers called Calvados "applejack," after the American spirit obtained by mixing apple spirit and neutral alcohol. They also called it "white lightning" because of its strength. So as to be able to stand appalling scenes, soldiers on both sides drank without any moderation. Many American GIs got their first taste of Calvados during the battle of Normandy.

Cider apple trees took their part in the battle by never showing who they favored. Antony Beevor, British historian and author of *D-Day: The Battle for Normandy*, reports a surprise attack of British tanks through orchards and hedges. the tanks' commanders got scratched by low branches in their faces and were bombed with tiny cider apples that accumulated in the turrets. He quotes a British tank commander: "In the small fields of Normandy among the cider orchards, every move during the hot summer brought showers of small hard sour apples cascading into the turrets through the open batches. After a few days there might be enough to jam the turret. Five men in close proximity, three in the turret and two below in the driving compartment, all in a thick metal oven, soon produced a foul smell: humanity, apples, cordite and heat."

Caught between the Germans and the Allies, farmers faced difficult situations they had to manage. Beevor relates a number of anecdotes, including the following — (perhaps true, perhaps fictional) of an American tank platoon pulling into a Norman farmyard. The farmer emerged with cider and Calvados and all the soldiers had a drink. Afterwards, the Norman farmer tells the young American lieutenant that the drinks come to 100 francs. The lieutenant protests that they have just liberated him. "But what are you complaining about?" the farmer replies. "It's no more than I charged the Germans."

Despite the plundering of local goods, the relationships between the locals and the Allied troops gradually became friendlier. However, many Norman people feared the Germans might come back — and for good reason. In Villers-Bocage, for example the inhabitants welcomed a British regiment — The Sharpshooters — ecstatically, offering presents of cider and butter. Yet, facing the German army's counter attack, the British had to withdraw before Royal Air Force bombers crushed Villers-Bocage, leaving a dreadful mess.

Calvados took part in the Battle of Normandy until the German army retreated. Beevor tells the story of German corporal Spiekerkötter and his small group running away from General Patton's column. They had hidden a small cask of Calvados under mines at the back of their lorry. Their officer, Lieutenant Nowack, met them on the green of a small village, discovered the keg and gave them a good hand to empty it. In high spirits, he held up his glass and shouted, "Calvados is still in the Germans' hands."

After the Armistice was signed, war prisoners came back home to be greeted with heavy meals showered with Calvados. Decades after the war ended, many veterans returned to Normandy with their families. In 1994, Normandy celebrated the 50th anniversary of D-Day, and thousands of veterans crossed the Atlantic to take part in the commemoration events. Norman people remembered what they owed the soldiers who had liberated them and welcomed them heartily.

To express our gratitude, I greeted many groups of veterans in our distillery with *good* Calvados, not the fiery welcome drink they got in 1944. Later, I was invited to the city of Tours by a friend of mine, Jacques Weber, who had been one of the chiefs of "La Résistance" in the Loire Valley. There, I attended a remembrance ceremony presided over by General George Patton IV, George Smith Patton's son. Jacques Weber introduced me to General Patton who told me he wanted to thank me for what I had done. I thought he was a bit confused and told him I was not yet born in 1944. He laughed and explained that veterans had told him how happy they were of the warm welcome they had received in our distillery and he wanted to thank me for that.

▶ The Role of War

Calvados Pays d'Auge became part of a small group of spirits protected by an Appellation d'Origine Contrôlée (AOC) in 1942, at the height of World War II and during France's occupation by Nazi Germany. The AOC is a recognition and protection producers aspire to. It constitutes the letters of nobility of a great product. As a rule, producers mobilize to obtain it without backing down from the considerable efforts required to justify the request. So, did the Normans have nothing more pressing on their minds, at such dark time in their history, than claiming a designation of origin for their spirit?

Calvados as Tank Fuel and Stills as Cannons

On January 13th, 1941, under pressure from the occupying authorities, the French government was forced to pass a law to deal with the shortage of fuel for war vehicles. As a result, the entire French production of spirits, including Calvados, was reserved for Service des Alcools, with the exception of brandies carrying an AOC. Only Cognac and Armagnac qualified as AOC at that time, escaping requisition. Stocks of Calvados and cider spirits not protected by a designation of origin were doomed to be converted into fuel for tanks and military vehicles. With Germans requisitioning all available copper for weapons production, how could their stills be saved?

Horrified at the thought of what would become of their spirit, the Normans appealed to the National Institute of Origin and Quality (INAO), which is tasked with ensuring the recognition and protection of official signs identifying the quality and origin of agricultural and food products. Although Baron Leroy, who was to become President of INAO, had suggested creating AOC categories for ciders, pear ciders, and cider spirits as early as 1923, nothing had been done at the time France went to war in 1939. Fortunately, INAO still retained jurisdiction and authority over cider spirits.

The French Minister of agriculture Jacques Le Roy Ladurie, who was of Norman origin, also wanted to protect the stock of Calvados. Cider spirit producers and their unions submitted the required reasons and proposals to INAO for regulation of cider spirit production. A study conducted between February and September of 1942 led to two decrees issued in 1942 which placed Calvados and cider spirits under a designation of origin scheme. Thus, the Normans obtained a designation of origin for their apple and pear spirits.

However, with no means to carry out proper investigation, geographical boundaries were initially established quite generously, with the main goal of preserving spirit from requisition. The protected area was huge, with very few restrictions. This first regulatory stage brought the production of Calvados within more reasonable geographical limits, but the future would show the need for more stringent regulations. The legal provisions were revised and improved in 1984 and 1997, and producers began to impose additional disciplines upon themselves to help create the Calvados of today.

▶ 1942: The First Recognition of Calvados as a Controlled Appellation.

The decrees of 1942 and 1947 established the initial controlled designation of origin for Calvados. The AOC was granted only to those products possessing distinctive and specific characteristics, and special notoriety. Calvados du Pays d'Auge was the only Calvados originally recognized as an *Appellation d'Origine Contrôlée*.

A new category of Appellation of Origin was created: Appellation Réglementée. Ten areas were initially allowed an Appellation Calvados d'Origine Réglementée, one of them being Domfrontais: Calvados du Calvados, Calvados du Cotentin, Calvados de l'Avranchin, Calvados du Domfrontais, Calvados de la Vallée de l'Orne, Calvados du Mortanais, Calvados du Pays du Merlerault, Calvados du Perche, Calvados du Pays de la Risle, and Calvados du Pays de Bray.

Three areas were acknowledged as Appellation réglementées : Eaux-de-vie de cidre" : Normandie, Maine and Bretagne.

The protection offered by an *Appellation d'Origine* also involves accepting INAO's supervision. This restriction is hardly compatible with the Norman character. Fiercely individualistic, Norman people will fight tooth and claw to defend their individual

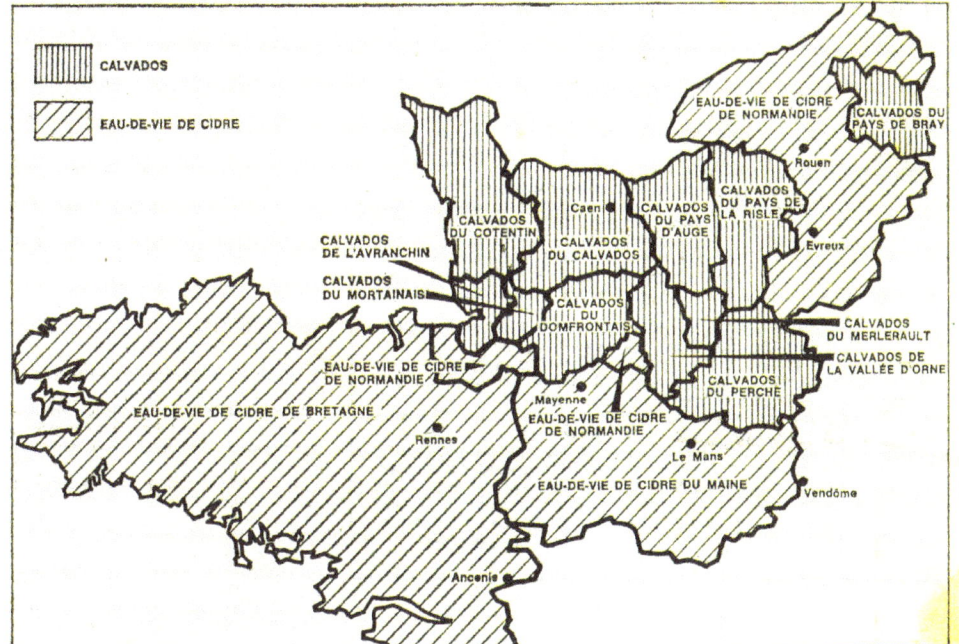

1942 map illustrating the recognition of Calvados as a controlled Appellation

freedoms. Why worry about *Appellation* regulations when fraud secures a good price and cash payment for just-out-of-the-still spirits?

Easy solutions, however, are never solutions for the future. The time was fast approaching when fraud would no longer pay and only quality would guarantee sales — provided it was promoted. If Calvados was to become a resource for producers and for Normandy, it had to be supported by stricter designations. Admittedly, creating them proved to be laborious, to say the least. More rigorous regulatory steps were set in 1984, 1998, and 2015.

▶ The 1984 Reform

The creation of the European Union raised the issue of protecting the designations of origin. The Northern states, initially hostile to designations of origin, which they considered a form of protectionism, eventually accepted them on condition that they had to be strictly justified and that only controlled designations would be protected. The vast area covered by the regulated names of Calvados and cider spirits, which included Normandy, Brittany and Maine, was not justifiable. INAO urgently started the first reform in 1984, hastily bringing together the 10 previously regulated Calvados designations to create a single *Appellation Calvados Contrôlée*. The Domfrontais region was invited but declined to apply for a specific AOC. Cider spirits were no longer protected.

▶ The 1998 Reform

Producers were soon asked to review the rules ruling their designations. The request was not opposed, as everyone was well aware of the need to fill the gaps left by the first decrees. After years of hard work, three controlled designations of origin were established in 1998: Calvados Pays d'Auge, Calvados Domfrontais, and Calvados. With the unwavering support of Jean Pinchon, President of INAO, the Domfrontais region finally applied for and obtained its own specific designation. This time, as all orchards had to be identified and approved, rigor won over laxity.

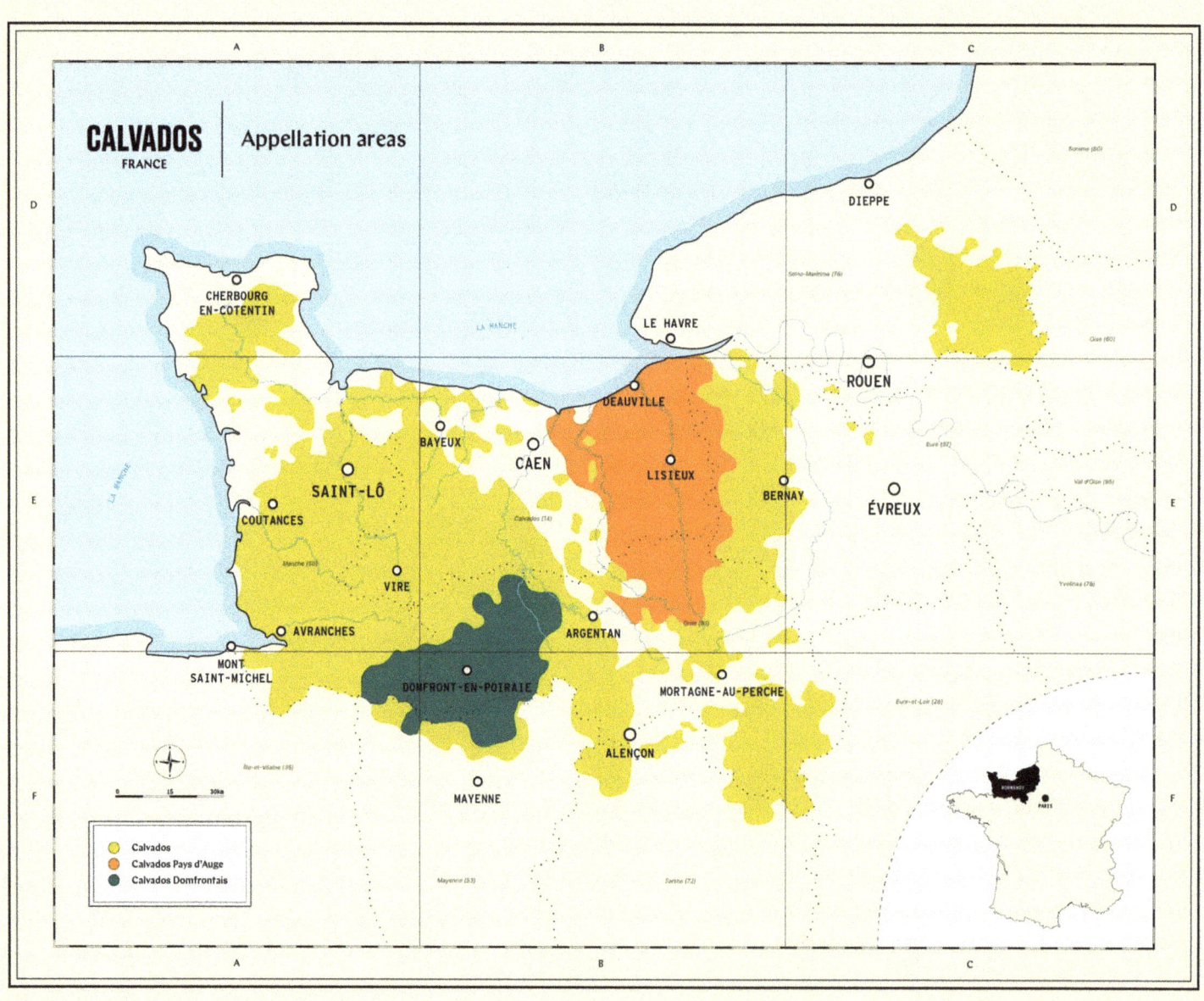

▸ The February 2015 Decrees

The rules applicable to the three designations were codified in the 2015 decrees, which once again made restrictions more stringent. From 1942 to 2015 we went from laxity to one of the most restrictive regulations.

▸ The Three Calvados Designations Today

The ultimate character of any Calvados is a combination of the soil, the fruit varieties used, the fermentation of the must, the distillation method, and the aging process.

For a long time, the role of soil was viewed only in terms of its physical and chemical characteristics, with no consideration for the life in the soil, even though the interaction between the microflora in the soil and the tree's root system is an essential factor in the expression of a terroir. A properly aerated soil helps the development of the root system, which enables the plant to firmly anchor to the ground and absorb the water and nutrients it needs. Fauna like bacteria, earthworms, and small animals are responsible for soil porosity, allowing air and water to penetrate deep into the ground, and microflora is responsible for forming the nutrients absorbed by the trees.

Until the 1970s, nothing hindered the expression of terroir in wine and cider production. Then came a revolution in agricultural practices that disrupted life in the soil: intensive agriculture. This revolution affected much of viticulture and offered vine-growers the opportunity to secure higher yields and save crops by using massive quantities of plant protection products, powerful pesticides, herbicides, and chemical fertilizers. These practices have wiped out the fauna, leading in some cases to total disappearance of biological activity. Nutrients can only form if the soil is well aerated by wildlife. With the disappearance of soil life, the nutrients that plants can no longer find in the soil need to be provided in the form of fertilizers. The connection with the soil is thus lost along with the expression of the terroir. Since the vine roots can no longer reach the bedrock, the resulting wine is no longer a terroir wine, but a varietal wine like any other.

The "pré-verger" system, which combines meadows and orchards, and the absence of chemical treatments make for a very active soil life. The revolution in agricultural practices has not affected fruit production in standard sized orchards, which predate the green revolution. In dwarf orchards, the use of chemicals has been limited and has not smothered soil life. As a result, Calvados producers never had to face the same problems as winemakers who adopted the so-called modern agricultural practices.

The relationship between soil, bacteria, and tree varieties is too complex to be replicated. By contributing to a product's specificity, a living soil also protects it from foreign competition and gives it a unique character. Many countries produce cider spirits, but none has managed to imitate Calvados. Some producers — mainly Americans — have imported cider apple trees from Normandy. They can produce excellent spirits which however will necessarily express a different terroir.

The fruit extracts an expression of the terroir from the soil that fermentation with wild yeasts, followed by distillation, turns into fragrances. When these fragrances reach the nostrils, the receptor cells send a message to the brain, which identifies them. Normally, the mouth merely confirms the information provided by the nose. A Designation of Origin product must express its terroir, revealing its soul.

Calvados has a fascinating, evocative power. It's a reflection of the country where it was made and the people who produced it. For those who are familiar with Pays d'Auge and Domfrontais — two regions with consistent, identifiable characteristics —the respective designations are easy to recognize. The expression of the terroir is strong. For the generic name Calvados, this is much more difficult as the production area, which covers eleven regions, many of which have their own specific characteristics, is extremely diverse.

Calvados Pays d'Auge
59 producers — 3,252 hectares

Created in 1942, Pays d'Auge is the oldest and most famous Calvados appellation and the first Appellation Contrôlée in Normandy. It produces Calvados that is mellow and full bodied. To carry the Pays d'Auge appellation, the Calvados must be made from cider produced exclusively using fruit harvested in Pays d'Auge, and may contain up to 30% pears.

Different types of soil can be identified in Pays d'Auge: clay and flint, clay and green chalk, clay and limestone, and silt. Clay, which is common throughout Pays d'Auge, offers ideal conditions for the shallow root system of apple trees. Pear trees are also found in Pays d'Auge, mostly in hedges protecting apple orchards. Pays d'Auge must be distilled twice in copper pot stills and aged for at least two years in oak casks.

Pays d'Auge has been known for centuries for its excellent dairy products and cider fruit. In 1588, historian Charles de Bourgueville wrote that "the whole Auge region is rich in fruit and apples, from which the most excellent ciders can be obtained." In addition to exceptional cream and butter, it also produces cheeses like Camembert, Livarot and Pont-L'Evêque which have enjoyed some fame.

Pays d'Auge is a very uniform area, both geographically and geologically. It includes four different natural areas: the coast, marshes, woods, and the *bocage*, an agricultural landscape of cultivated regions divided by regular hedges and banks. The *bocage* has strongly eroded elevations — a succession of hills and valleys divided into small plots that give it its unique charm. Those used for grazing cows under apple trees are enclosed by hedges.

Horse breeding, especially racehorses, is a rapidly developing industry. In recent decades, an increase in the number of horse stables has changed the landscape, with a larger number of treeless plots enclosed by wooden or concrete fences. The soils are predominantly made of clay with a silty surface layer. Heavy, cold soils combined with the mild, humid climate are ideal for grazing land and apple farming, but are not immune to global warming and its consequences.

After World War I, André du Boullay, a producer, lamented the absence of an organization capable of protecting Camembert and Calvados, which had become public domain. As early as 1922 he decided to devote his efforts to defending farmers and bringing them together into a union. The "Syndicat de la Marque d'Origine Pays d'Auge" was created in 1926 with the goal of certifying the origin of top Auge products. Together with other industry players, the Syndicat applied for an *Appellation d'Origine Contrôlée* for Calvados produced in Pays d'Auge. To mark the boundaries of the Pays d'Auge terroir, the union hired a geographer, Marcel Reinhard. The 1942 decree adopted the same demarcation, with slightly expanded borders.

Today, the Pays d'Auge designation is regulated by the 2015 decree. Fruit production and picking, the production and distillation of apple and pear cider, and the ageing process must all take place within the geographical area defined in the decree. An annex lists the municipalities included in this geographical area.

Another annex specifies the permitted cider fruit varieties. Seventy percent of the surface area must be planted with bitter and bittersweet varieties. The decree also stipulates the requirements for the management of high- and low-stem orchards and yields per hectare. At least 45% of the fruit used at each production site must come from high-stem orchards. No more than 30% of the cider to be distilled may come from cider pears.

Distillation takes place in stills with a maximum capacity of 2500 liters. The first distillation consists of boiling the cider, which contains about 6% alcohol, to obtain the *petite eau*, which has an alcohol content between 28% to 30%. The second distillation - or *bonne chauffe* - involves the *petites eaux* obtained from the first distillation. The result is unaged Calvados, which must have an ABV not exceeding 72%. The first and last distillation products, or the "heads" and "tails," are discarded and only the hearts are used. To obtain the designation, the spirit must age for no less than 24 months in sessile or pedunculate oak barrels. Barrel capacity is also regulated.

In my opinion, what sets Pays d'Auge Calvados apart is its smooth apple aromas; the fullness, roundness, and fatness of the mouth; and, after prolonged ageing, the balance, mellowness, richness, and extreme complexity of the aromas and flavors. Calvados Pays d'Auge reflects the region, with its soft cheeses and cuisine rich in cream and butter — a land loved for its gently rolling landscapes and the understated class of its half-timbered buildings.

Calvados Domfrontais
52 producers — 752 hectares

Like Pays d'Auge, the Domfrontais region is quite uniform both geographically and geologically. Discreetly tucked away in southern Normandy between Alençon and Mont-Saint-Michel, the Domfrontais *bocage* is a rolling wooded region of hills and ridges, with rugged terrain and an abundance of waterholes. The fields and meadow orchards are bordered by hedges and coppices. Dairy cattle farming and cider, perry, and calvados production are the main agricultural activities of the *bocage* region. However, corn farming is on the rise.

Despite a considerable decline in its orchards, what still impresses visitors to the Domfrontais are the tall, imposing trees standing majestically in the natural meadows. The pear tree is a very slow-growing tree that reaches adulthood at fifty years of age and can live for several centuries. These large pear trees bloom before the apple trees. In fall, in favorable years, the pear trees fill with small green or grey pears that are used to produce *poiré*, a sparkling drink similar to cider.

The pear tree is the signature of Domfrontais Calvados. The ubiquity of pear trees here is due to the nature of the soil, which promotes their growth. It is a deep soil consisting of a granite bedrock and shale layers covered with silt, with good water retention. The soil is well aerated by microorganisms and the biological activity next the bedrock helps create elements that can be absorbed by the trees and are specific to this terroir, which contributes to making this product unique.

The most important feature of Calvados produced in the Domfrontais region is its nose, unmistakable in the world of spirits with its elegance, finess, and enticing scent of pears. It is often more vibrant than the Calvados produced in Pays d'Auge. Pays d'Auge and Domfrontais Calvados are two aristocratic spirits: one smooth, rich, full-bodied, unfathomable; the other wild and fiery.

The specifications for the Calvados Domfrontais designation require that cider pears make up at least 30% of the fruit used, and that the resulting spirit be aged in oak barrels for at least three years. The specifications also define the geographical area (a total of 1600 km^2) and list the 114 municipalities it covers. At least 80% of the orchards must be planted with high-stem trees. The permitted apple and pear varieties are specified in an annex. The percentage of *poiré* pear trees planted must be at least 25%. The percentage of bitter and bitter-sweet apple trees must be at least 70%. Allowable yields are also specified.

The distillation method contributes to the character of the spirit. In the Domfrontais region, Calvados is traditionally produced in column stills that turn cider into alcohol through a continuous process. The column still is excellent for extracting apple and pear aromas, giving the spirit unique aromatic exuberance, freshness, and liveliness. This distillation method is mandatory to obtain the Domfrontais AOC. Cider and *poiré* are distilled together in a column still. After distillation, the eau-de-vie must not exceed 72% ABV.

Calvados Domfrontais must age in sessile or pedunculate oak barrels. Barrel capacity is also regulated. To preserve the fruit aromas as much as possible, producers seldom use new barrels. Unfortunately, a minimum ageing of three years is required for Calvados Domfrontais. As its fruity aromas make it ideal to be enjoyed young, either straight or in cocktails, a large amount of Calvados made in Domfrontais is placed on the market before three years of age under the Calvados designation.

Calvados AOC
337 producers — 7,329 hectares

The *Appellation Calvados Contrôlée* covers the largest production area, with very diverse soil types. The selected municipalities are those in which traditional cider production had been maintained, stemming from traditional orchards combining fruit trees with grazing grass for livestock. *Appellation Calvados Contrôlée* can be produced in both Pays d'Auge and Domfrontais if all of the obligations for these specific designations are not met.

The requirements for the production of Calvados are less stringent. The respective ratios of cider apples and pears are not regulated, although 70% of the apples must be from bitter or bittersweet varieties. At least 35% of all fruit used must come from high-stem orchards. Apple or pear ciders are distilled in pot stills or column stills. As the production cost of double distillation is higher than the cost of single column distillation, only a few producers use the former. The spirit must age for at least two years in sessile or pedunculate oak barrels.

Since production of *Appellation Calvados Contrôlée* can vary quite widely across the region, it's difficult to perceive the bond with the terroir, and even more difficult to pinpoint the specificities of the Calvados produced here. Therefore, the very brief description of this designation characteristics as provided in the production specifications is quite appropriate: "The nose and mouth are aromatic with notes reminiscent of the fruit from which it's obtained." This does not in any way affect the quality of the product, which some producers have successfully taken to very high levels.

Calvados production meets all of the requirements of a true designation of origin. By nurturing soil life in their orchards, the Normans have successfully preserved the expression of their terroir in Calvados.

The Defense
TRAVELING DISTILLERS
DISTILLATION COOPERATIVES AND HARVESTERS

Producing Calvados

CALVADOS IS A CIDER SPIRIT produced in Normandy. The main stages of production are:

- Growing cider apples and perry pears
- Harvesting apples and pears
- Mashing and pressing fruits into must
- Fermenting the must into cider
- Distilling the cider
- Aging calvados in oak barrels

There are no secrets in the production of Calvados, but at each step of the process, distillers must make decisions that balance considerations of quality, cost, and style. Each primary stage is described in detail in this chapter.

▶ Growing Cider Apples and Perry Pears

Apple and pear varieties, terroir, climate and history all play a role in shaping today's Norman orchards. Calvados differs from some other apple spirits as it is produced by distilling fermented apple juice rather than fermented apples. It also differs from other cider-based spirits made from table apples. What makes Calvados unique is the use of specific apple and pear varieties, all specially grown for producing apple and pear cider. These are different from their table counterparts, which are not allowed for the production of Calvados as they are low in tannins (polyphenols).

Apple and Pear Varieties

There are many apple brandies/cider spirits in the world, but none enjoy a better reputation than Calvados. What makes Calvados so unique are the apple and pear varieties that are grown exclusively for the production of cider in Normandy. With few exceptions, like the English Somerset Cider Brandy or the Aguardientes di Sidra produced in Asturias, most of the world's cider spirits are produced from table apples and, as a result, show much less character and complexity than Calvados.

Dwarf or low stem apple trees

About 7,500 hectares (around 18,500 acres) of cider apple and perry pear orchards are grown in Normandy. They consist of hundreds of varieties, including many that can be traced back to at least the 19th century. Each variety is classified into one of several main categories according to their flavor and seasonality: bitter, bittersweet, sweet, acidic; and early, mid-season, and late. Bitter apples are rich in tannin and provide body. Bittersweet apples are also rich in tannin, but are higher in sugar. Sweet apples are higher in sugar, lower in tannin and acidity, and contribute to raising the alcohol content in cider. Acidic apples are low in tannin and deliver more fruitiness, but tend to produce sharper-tasting spirits. Calvados can also be produced from perry pears, which tend to be more acidic than apples. Some of the many named varieties of Norman cider apples include Bedan, Binet Rouge, Fréquin Rouge, Clos Renaux, Noël des Champs, and Peau de Chien. Norman perry pears include Plant de Blanc, Fausset, Rouge Vigné, Gros Blot, and Planc roux.

These apples deliver a great range of flavors and aromatic intensity. Production specifications list the apple varieties that can be used for each of the three controlled Calvados appellations: Calvados, Calvados Pays d'Auge, and Calvados Domfrontais. Producers of Calvados Pays d'Auge can choose from 103 apple and 30 pear varieties selected for their richness in polyphenols and other specific agronomic qualities. Between 15 and 40 different varieties are found in most orchards. Orchards planted after 1997 must include a maximum of 10% acidic and a minimum of 70% polyphenol-rich bitter and bittersweet apple varieties.

This mix of varieties serves an agronomic purpose as well as a gustatory one. Normandy is prone to spring frosts, which can have dramatic consequences on blooming and fruit formation. Yet, as each of these apple varieties blooms at different times over a period of six weeks, it is extremely rare for all of them to be affected by frost. Mixing early, mid-season, and late varieties also helps better distribute work in the orchard. Depending on the apple variety, harvest takes place between late September and early December each year.

Standard Versus Dwarf Orchards

Since the 1980s, the traditional combination of lovely orchards of standard-sized apple trees (*hautes tiges,* or high stem) with pasture beneath has been giving way to orchards of dwarf or low stem apple trees. This change has been encouraged by cider industrialists as well as French administration advocates of intensive agriculture.

Dwarf orchards are devoted exclusively to the production of fruit. Here, the grass is not cropped by cows but mown by machines so as to form a lawn which will cushion the fall of the apples. Most dwarf orchards were planted for contractual supply of industrial cideries. Standard trees are planted to around 100 plants per hectare, on average, while dwarf trees are planted to 550-800 trees per hectare. Traditional orchards are fully productive after 18 years and have approximately 70 years of life expectancy, while intensive dwarf orchards are fully productive after eight years and their life expectancy is 30-35 years. Dwarf orchards give a better return on investment and have better resistance to storms. Yet the trees are fragile and more subject to diseases and insect attacks. For traditional orchards, the yield should not be more than 25 tons per hectare, and for dwarf orchards, no more than 35 tons per hectare.

Orchards and Carbon Capture

Those who come to Normandy for the first time expect to find Norman cows grazing peacefully under apple and pear trees – a beautiful scene widely celebrated by novelists, painters, and magazine reports. How many times have I greeted visitors who, as they got off the train at Pont-L'Evêque station, told me how astonished they were at seeing no sign of the legendary Norman orchards through the window. The reason for this is that orchards have now been partly replaced by corn fields, and many of the traditional standard tree orchards have been replaced by dwarf varieties.

The significant decline of orchards due to the loss of a number of key markets for cider and Calvados doesn't just damage the magnificence of the landscape. Apple and pear orchards also contribute to preserving biodiversity as well as fighting climate change. The issue of biodiversity has become a major concern today. As standard apple and pear trees are hardy and highly resistant to disease, chemical treatments are not needed, which helps protect biodiversity. Traditional orchards are also full-fledged ecosystems. The soil is alive with microorganisms and worms that turn everything they ingest into fertilizer of exceptional quality. Bees promote pollination, the ideal number being two beehives per hectare. Tits and sparrows protect fruits by keeping the insect population in check. Hedges provide birds with shelter, and nesting boxes helps increase their number. Cows graze the grass and fertilize the soil.

At Christian Drouin, we take other steps to protect the environment. We source all of our fruit from within a range of just 15 kilometers. Our bottles and cartons are produced within 200 kilometers of the distillery. The still is equipped with a next-generation gas burner to limit consumption. A cider heater recovers some of the heat created during distillation.

Preserving traditional know-how rooted in common sense and natural production methods makes it possible to produce one of the most virtuous spirits on the planet. Our orchard, which is planted exclusively with standard size apple trees and surrounded by hedges, is a case in point. One hectare of cider apple orchard absorbs 5.3 tons of CO_2, nearly the same amount as one hectare of forest, while one hectare of cereal for making whisky absorbs 2 tons, one hectare of sugar cane absorbs 1.8 tons, and one hectare of vineyard absorbs approximately one ton. As we recently found out while assessing Christian Drouin's Calvados carbon footprint, after considering gas consumption for distillation, electricity consumption, glass, and cardboard packaging as well as transportation and shipping, each bottle of Calvados produced removes 2.9 kg of CO_2 from the atmosphere.

And nothing prevents Calvados producers using fruit from standard trees from going even further to reduce their carbon footprint. To our knowledge, no other spirit can contribute to the fight against global warming as much as Calvados. The carbon balance is not just neutral, it is definitely positive. Given the magnitude of the climate change emergency, any effort to reduce carbon pollution should be applauded and promoted. Calvados might well be the world's most sustainable spirit.

▸ Harvest

The annual harvest takes place from late September to the beginning of December, depending on apple varieties. Mixes of early, middle, and late maturing varieties enable the family to spread out the work. We only harvest apples that fall naturally from the tree, or those that fall after shaking the tree.

The apples should reach their optimum point of maturity before being pressed. Traditionally, in Norman farms, the apples were kept in the attic to reach perfect ripeness. If one does not have a dry, aerated place for fruit to finish ripening, one has to pick only the fruit that has fallen on the ground — that is to say, those that are perfectly ripe, making it necessary to make multiple passages under each tree. Today, the apples that fall on the ground are mostly picked up by machines. This is easier than harvesting by hand, but multiple passes still considerably increase the cost of harvesting. This is the price for quality.

▸ Mashing

Mature fruit must be washed, crushed, and pressed. The apples and pears are washed by floating them in water. They are then run up a conveyor belt to the top of the grinder. Rotten apples are removed manually while they move along the belt. As the fruits are very hard, they must be shred or crushed into a fine pulp before being pressed. Do not expect Norman farmers to trample apples or pears with their feet!

Left, hydraulic press, center and right, pneumatic press.

As most of Calvados's flavor is extracted from the skin, the fruits should not be peeled or cored before crushing. The pulpy mass of crushed apples is called the mash. The most primitive way of crushing fruits was in a mortar with a pestle. Then came the horse-mill: a large, circular trough of stone or wood with a big inset stone or wooden wheel turned by a horse. Nowadays, this step is performed mechanically with a grinder.

▶ Pressing

There are different types of presses to extract the juice from the pomace. By the eighteenth century, screw presses with massive wooden screws were popular. These are now relics of the past visible in museums. They preceded the iron screw, which appeared in the 19th century: the press had a central iron screw and a square or round squeezer base. Then, at the beginning of the 20th century, hydraulic pack presses replaced this type of press. Today, small producers often use a mobile hydraulic pack press transported to the estate, while others have their own hydraulic pack press with racks and cloths.

In a hydraulic pack press, the pulp is dumped onto a cloth set into a rack, and the corners of the cloth are folded into the center, enveloping the pulp. Another rack is placed on top of it and the same procedure is repeated until six to 10 layers are built up. When pressed, the juice flows through the cloth. Pressure should be applied slowly and regularly to ensure quality. The manual nature of pressing in this way means that more labor is required.

The pneumatic press is more effective. Once limited to large producers, the pneumatic press is now more affordable to smaller producers. In a pneumatic press, the pulp is pumped into a stainless-steel container. The producer then fills a membrane, which compresses air and presses the juice out gently and evenly.

If the objective of a producer is to produce at low cost, he will extract as much juice as possible from the fruit. But for superior quality it is better not to press too hard so as to leave most of the seeds intact. Between 600 and 750 liters of juice are extracted from

one ton of apples. If you extract 600 liters from one ton of apples, and produce cider at 5.5% alcohol, it takes 21 kilograms of fruit to produce 1 liter of Calvados at 70% alcohol —that's how much work goes into a bottle.

Once the pulp is pressed, the solid part called marc is separated and — most of the time — given to livestock. But if quantities are important, after drying, marc is sent to a specialized factory to have pectin extracted and sold as an ingredient to thicken jams, fruit pastes, sauces, and other products.

The juice pressed from the crushed apple pulp is allowed to stand in vats until impurities rise to the top. Then the clear liquid at the bottom is drained off and fermented.

▶ Fermentation

Cider is a beverage born of the slow fermentation of cider apple juice during the winter.

Pressed apple and pear juice contains natural sugar and yeast, including airborne yeast present in the cellar and yeast from the skin of the fruit. During fermentation, yeast consumes and breaks down the natural sugar and transforms it into alcohol.

The juice ferments naturally for a period ranging from six weeks to a few months, depending on cellar temperature, as yeast is less active at cold temperatures. When fermentation is completed, the end result is dry cider. Distilling cider must have an alcohol content of at least 4.5% (most are between 5-6% and some are over 7%). Volatile acidity must be under 2.5 grams per liter and no sugar can be added. Distilling cider less than three weeks old is not allowed in Normandy.

Today, most producers ferment their ciders in stainless steel tanks to keep it fresh. But traditionally, fermentation took place in cement tanks or large wooden vats or barrels. In order to avoid emptying the vat too soon and taking the risk of dry staves, farmers used to empty their cider casks for distillation only when the next year's vintage cider was produced. This meant that all distilled cider was about a year old.

By experimenting with the distillation of different kinds of cider, we have found that cider's age has quite a strong influence on the taste of the Calvados produced. Young

cider tends to evolve into smooth, round, and fruity spirits, ideal for making La Blanche or young blends. Distillation of older ciders leads to more complex Calvados with higher acidity and volatility. These are the ones that evolve perfectly after a long period of aging and evaporation.

▸ Distillation

The distiller, heir to alchemists, exposes cider to flames. In Pays d'Auge, they use pot stills. In Domfrontais and other parts of Normandy, they use column stills. In either case, the distiller cuts the heads and tails to keep only the heart, the *coeur de chauffe*, a colorless, ardent, scented eau-de-vie we call *la blanche*.

In Calvados, the distillation year begins on July 1st and ends on June 30th of the next year. Distillation consists of separating the alcohol from the water. When cider is heated with either gas or a woodfire, alcohol, whose boiling point is lower than that of water, evaporates first. The vapors containing the alcohol are then collected and condensed. Through distillation, we can extract the complex aromas of the cider.

In the Pays d'Auge AOC, cider must be double-distilled in a copper pot still. During the second run, the first and last parts of the run (the heads and the tails) are separated from the heart of the distillation and recycled into the next batch. Thus, production consists of two stages: the extraction of "petites eaux" (which contain 28% to 30% alcohol) followed by their transformation into spirit (which contains between 69% and 72% alcohol.)

Mobile column still at the Verger Normand winery in Domfront.

In Domfrontais AOC and most of Calvados AOC, cider is distilled once in continuous column stills equipped with three taps to separate the heads and tails from the heart. The still is made of three parts: the boiler, the column, and the condensation column. Domfrontais Calvados must be single distilled. Calvados AOC permits single or double distillation, although most producers opt for single distillation. But not all. Although it costs more, the Caboulet family of Domaine des Hauts Vents in Saint-Ouen–du-Tilleul relies on double distillation process to produce Calvados AOC.

Years ago, there were thousands of distillers in Normandy, and most Norman farmers produced Calvados. Today, however, fewer than 300 distillers exist, and the largest five producers are responsible for about 85% of total sales and 95% of exports.

Some agricultural distillers have their own press and still, while others resort to the historic tradition of a mobile distiller coming with his travelling still. The distiller parks his still in the farmyard near a water point, pond, or river. My father, Christian Drouin senior, started the production of his Calvados by calling on a legendary travelling distiller: Pierre Pivet. He bought that still from Pivet when he retired, and, for many years, the

ALAMBIC double distillation

Operating diagram of column still

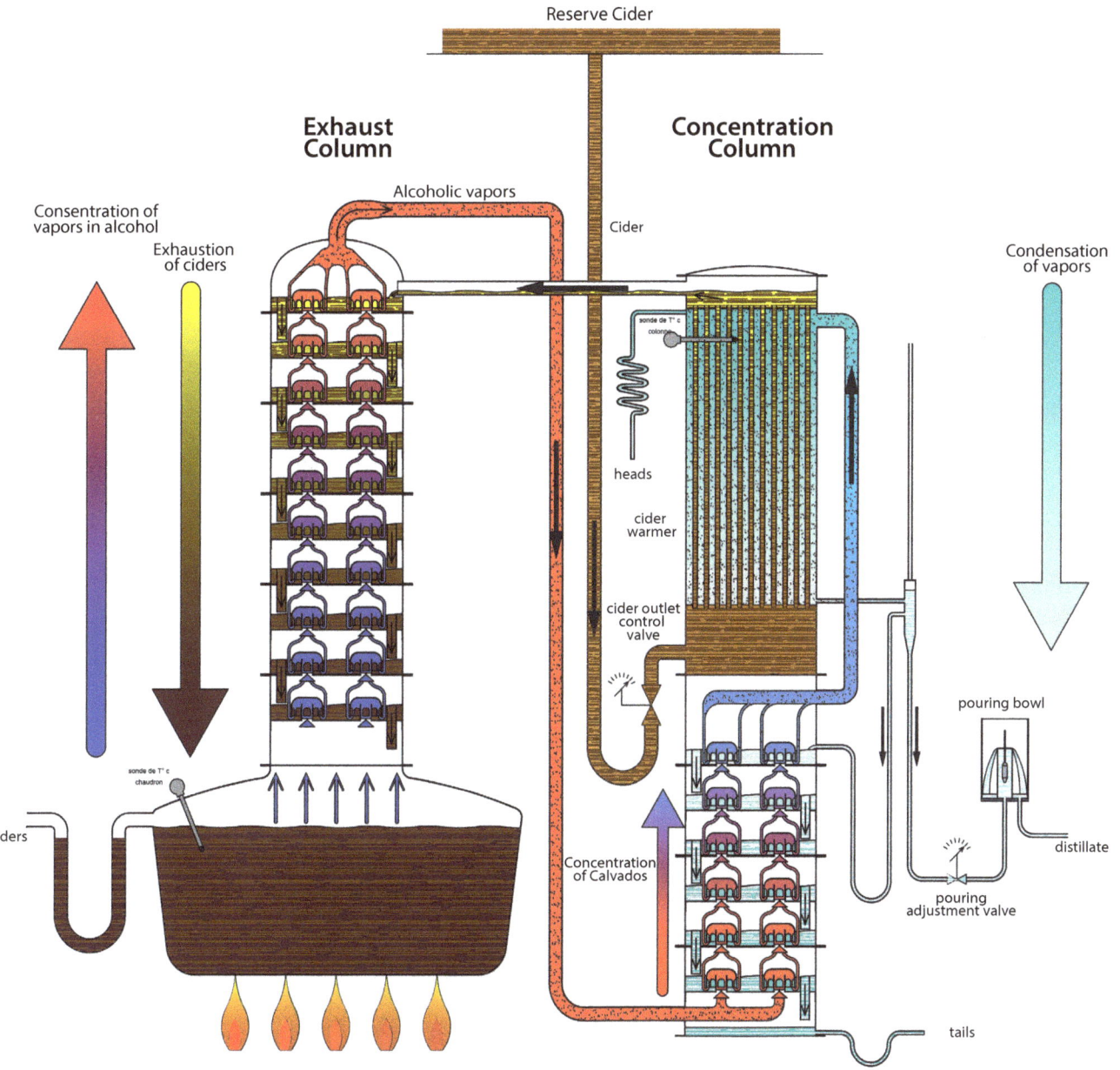

Drouin House produced its Calvados with this former travelling pot still. Today, it stands in the middle of the distillery courtyard in testimony of the past. Distillers no longer crisscross the countryside. The same goes for mobile cider makers who went from farm to farm to extract the juice from apples using their mobile press. They are disappearing at the same rate as the agricultural distillers.

▸ Aging

When it leaves the still, Calvados is colorless. It has an alcohol content between 69% and 72%, and cannot be sold as Calvados until it has been matured in oak barrels for at least two years (three years for calvados Domfrontais).

When time comes to age Calvados in oak casks, it's important to remember that the casks should not be treated simply as aging vessels, but also as flavoring agents, and skillfull aging is the art of matching spirit and oak. Oak is as much a part of Calvados as terroir or apple and pear varieties. Calvados extracts various substances from the wood, one of them being tannins which give color and body. On contact with oxygen, various wood compounds dissolved in the spirit undergo chemical transformation. The most volatile compounds which might give a young spirit a hot or burning taste disappear with time. Aging in oak barrels also introduces new aromas, which explains why the oldest Calvados, which spend the most time in oak, are the most complex.

The cask choice is, therefore, one of the most important decisions in the process. Matching Calvados with the right kind of oak is the challenging responsibility of the cellar master. Managing a portfolio of casks is complex and requires experience in order to understand them. Large producers have a cellar master on staff, but artisans and farmers are their own cellar master. Cask management will be different depending on the final objective. To lower costs, a producer competing primarily on prices and supplying mass distribution will conduct a different aging policy than producers supplying higher-end restaurants, bars, and retailers.

When you look for the perfect match, you have to understand the influence of wood on Calvados and conduct various experiments. Each cask develops differently. Calvados of the same batch aged in ten similar casks will give ten different products after a few years. To understand what a specific cask does to Calvados, you must frequently taste

Old cider barrels in the cave of Pierre Huet. Photo by Julien Boisard

the contents because what the wood delivers changes over the years. My son Guillaume and I taste every cask at least once a year. Knowing our casks inside out coupled with our experience enables us to deliver what we want to deliver.

Depending on a cellar master's desired effect, oak aging can take place in small casks or big ones, in new oak or old oak, and in European oak of various origins. Other factors, such as manufacturing techniques and toasting treatments, also influence different flavors and aromas. Small casks enable more exchange between the spirit and the wood to take place, which results in an acceleration of aging, with the drawback of greater losses through evaporation (otherwise known as the angels' share). For its initial fill, Calvados may be matured in fresh, unused oak casks containing concentrated flavor compounds. New casks can be fine if the wood has dried enough to eliminate green tannins. Otherwise, tannins disguise the fruit aromas. As Calvados is a fruit spirit appreciated for its apple and pear aromas, some producers prefer used casks that have previously held wine. They buy them from top wineries that use quality casks, and then send them to the cooper, who scratches the inside surface and toasts the cask again. When possible, they fill them with fresh cider to season them for a few months before filling them with freshly distilled Calvados.

An old tradition in Normandy, which had almost disappeared and has come back thanks to recent trendy specific casks finishes, is to use former sherry, Madeira and Port casks because they don't yield any bitter tannins and help give the spirit a finer color, more body, and greater aromatic richness. These fortified wines used to be imported to the region in casks and bottled in the ports of Le Havre or Rouen, where the empty casks were available at cheap prices. They were very popular with farmers because of their price and the positive influence that had on aging Calvados.

These casks reigned supreme until a change in the law required all sherry to be bottled in Spain, followed by Scotch whisky producers deciding to finish large quantities of whisky in sherry barrels. The demand for former sherry casks began to far exceeded the worldwide consumption of sherry. Some producers are now making sherry simply for the purpose of seasoning barrels.

Traditionally, sherry casks were made from European oak. More recently, some sherry producers have used former bourbon casks made from American oak. Only sherry casks made from European oak can be used for aging Calvados. There are different types of sherry, including oloroso and amontillado. In 1991, when sherry was still imported in bulk, our cooper Marius Duchemin advised us to buy a batch of high-quality casks previously used to age amontillado Sherry, which enabled us to win a good number of gold medals in major spirits competitions. Other kinds of casks that add a world of flavors to matured Calvados include cognac casks, fortified wines casks, Pommeau de Normandie casks, and former dessert wines casks that held wines such as French Sauternes or Hungarian Tokay.

Large vessels made from old wood are simply aging containers, and don't impart flavors from the wood. The wood is worn out, but it enables the oxidation process to go on. Such barrels are used to keep old Calvados, or as marrying vessels for preparing blends. Most Calvados producers specializing in old spirits favor the use of old casks, whereas those selling mostly young Calvados prefer using a high proportion of new casks and keep them from ten to fifteen years.

Adding caramel to achieve color consistency has always been a standard practice. However, a growing number of educated consumers are now aware that young spirit might be pale yellow and that each cask gives a different color. They become increasingly suspicious when the color seems too dark for the assumed age and suspect added ingredients. If the Calvados was perfectly distilled, there is no need to add any sugar, as it is smooth enough. It is likely to be a matter of time before labeling regulations oblige producers to stipulate the use of added ingredients.

▶ Bottling

To achieve consistency of aged blends, you must mix Calvados of complementary qualities. It is of the utmost importance to thoroughly know each of your barrels if you want to release vintages with unique character or limited editions of Calvados with specific characteristics (cask finish, cask strength, etc.). Artisan producers are proud of releasing unique small batches of products.

Today, there's a growing demand for spirits to be bottled in their most natural form. I am asked quite often whether we are allowed to add caramel, sugar, or wood extracts to Calvados. Such practices are still usual, as consumers often think the darker the better and producers want to achieve color consistency. Because each cask used for aging is unique, significant differences in the color of the contents can appear after a few years, even if casks are of the same type and filled with the same batch of Calvados.

Other issues raised by connoisseurs are chill filtering and bottling at cask strength. Traditionally, aged spirits were bottled after a light filtration at room temperature to eliminate foreign elements like dust or barrel char. The product was shipped perfectly clear, without sediments. Calvados, like other brown spirits, may later develop a haze in the bottle, in particular when exposed to low temperature. This may also happen when served chilled, or when water or ice is added. Heavy filtration will not solve the problem and will eliminate some interesting aromas.

Although such haze does not affect the quality of the spirit, consumers can misinterpret it as a sign of poor quality. To solve the problem, chill filtering has become a standard practice since the 1960s. In chill filtering, the spirit is cooled to precipitate certain organic molecules and then filtered to eliminate them before bottling. Not all producers chill filter, and those who do it filter at temperatures ranging from 17°F to 42°F in order to eliminate components that might solidify. Whether this chill filtering affects the experience of tasting in a positive or negative way is not clear.

In old times, Norman farmers enjoyed their Calvados without any water added. Today, Calvados is usually bottled with an alcohol content between 40% ABV and 43% ABV. During the aging process, the alcohol strength diminishes very slowly. To bring the alcohol down around 40-43%, pure water must be added to dilute it. When I started taking care of Calvados, Pierre Pivet instructed me that the water should be the age of the Calvados, and recommended lowering the alcohol strength significantly when the spirit is young because it mixes much better than older spirit. Indeed, adding a lot of water to old spirit just before bottling makes the Calvados taste flat and soapy. The disadvantage of reducing young Calvados' strength is that you need more casks to age the water, and this is costly.

Some consumers believe they get more of the original flavors if the spirit is tasted at cask strength. If your palate is able to taste spirits at 55% ABV or more, it might perceive some aromas better than others. As the cellar master tastes hundreds of Calvados batches every year, he is in a situation to understand the influence of alcoholic strength on aroma perception. Cask strength does not mean no water has been added. Calvados produced at 70% ABV will probably show an alcoholic strength of 64%ABV twenty years later without having any water added. Most producers start water reduction during the aging process, thus further lowering the alcohol strength. Therefore, cask strength means bottling without adding water just before bottling. To supply a demand of a small connoisseurs' category, some producers now release limited-edition bottlings of cask strength Calvados.

▸ **Label Terminology**

Control of aging is overseen by IDAC, which guarantees the age and authenticates the regulatory names. You may notice the following terms on bottles of Calvados:

Blended Calvados: The age indicated on the label is the age of the youngest component of the blend.

Trois Étoiles, Trois Pommes, VS (Very Special): Aged more than two years in oak barrels.

Vieux, Réserve: Aged more than three years.

Vieille Réserve, VO (Very Old), VSOP (Very Superior Old Pale): Aged more than four years.

Hors d'Age, XO, Extra, Age Inconnu, Très Vieux, Très Vieille Réserve: Aged more than six years.

Vintage: The vintage is the year of distillation. Traditionally, fruits are harvested in the fall, cider ferments during the winter and distillation is done the following year. For example, a 1980 vintage Calvados is produced from fruits harvested in 1979. If fermentation is completed before the end of the year, the distillation may take place in the same year. A producer may also keep his cider one more year in barrel before distilling it. Producers are allowed to sell vintages as long as they are able to prove that 100% of the content of the bottle was distilled in the year specified on the label. Controls are very strict.

Calvados fermier: The indication of "Calvados fermier" on a label indicates that the farmer produces Calvados exclusively from fruits grown on his farm.

▶ Other Norman Apple and Pear Products

Cider

Normandy is famous for its cider, whose complexity stems from the blend of cider apple varieties. It is an intensely flavored, deep colored, and refreshing beverage whose reputation has crossed the oceans. Cider is a versatile product that you can enjoy any time: if one gets thirsty in the afternoon, as an aperitif, with meals, with pancakes, in cocktails, and even as an ingredient in food. Festive, low in alcohol, gluten-free, and with the image of a natural product, cider has become increasingly trendy all over the world.

Unfortunately, authentic craft apple cider is difficult to produce, as its fermentation process is not easy to control. Most farmers are unable to explain why their cider was great in a specific year and disappointing the next year. I personally find it more challenging to produce cider than Calvados. To improve consistency in taste, one solution is to pasteurize the cider, which also makes it easier to travel. With unpasteurized cider, the problem lies in the difficulty to control fermentation once it's in the bottle. Cider may turn into an exceptional beverage as it may develop flavors that Norman people are used to, but which may taste strange to other people who are less familiar with them.

I have never felt comfortable with fermentations. I used to produce a small quantity of cider mainly for the visitors of the distillery, with a few cases exported to the United States. On December 24, 2003, came a huge surprise: *The New York Times* published a full page on "the worldwide revival of cider making." The panel tasted 21 ciders, including 11 from the United States, seven from France, and one each from England, Ireland, and Austria: "The cider from France swept the tasting, taking the top three spots and four of the top six. The Christian Drouin, our overall favorite, came from the Pays d'Auge, Calvados country and had great depth. The flavors of apples, earth and mint went on and on," wrote Eric Asimov.

Pears on truck bed at Louis de Lauriston

My son, Guillaume, an agronomist engineer from Montpellier school, was familiar with wine production. He was very excited at the idea of developing the production of cider and encouraged by countless requests for information from all over the world. He quickly realized cider fermentation was different from that of wine, and rather difficult. It was only after a few years of trial and error that he felt confident enough to work on a broader scale.

Pear Cider

In the south of Normandy they produce cider from pears. Pear cider or perry, known here as poiré, was called the "Champagne of Normandy" in the nineteenth century. It is a light, elegant, refreshing, slightly acidic sparkling drink.

It should be served chilled in a champagne flute. It can be enjoyed any time, as an aperitif, or with seafood,. Unfortunately, perry is even more difficult to produce than craft ciders, quantities are limited, and quality products are rare. Indeed, pears tend to rot very quickly after harvest, which imposes on producers to press the fruits within a few days.

La Blanche

"In the country one small glass of Blanche is the compulsory companion to coffee."
— Vieux mangers vieux parlers bas normands, Jean Seguin, 1934.

La Blanche is the un-aged version of the spirit used to make Calvados. Un-aged Calvados is not a new category. In 1942, no minimum aging was required for Calvados. In those days, Calvados distilled on a farm used to be farmers' everyday drink, and Blanche was the name given to the unaged cider spirit. Even if they stored their spirit in a barrel, it was not aged.

Another popular way of drinking Blanche in a French bistro until World War II was "Fine à l'eau," one of Commissaire Maigret's favorite drinks. It simply meant adding seltzer water to a brandy: Cognac, Armagnac or Calvados. These traditions may have disappeared, but the desire to work with the product is still alive and well.

In the late 1990s, French bartenders expressed their desire to work with "white Calvados" so as to prevent any coloring of the cocktail and to evoke well-developed cider apple aromas with no wood tannin. Peter Colin Field, the chief bartender of Bar Hemingway at Ritz Hotel in Paris, is one of the bartenders who talked me into producing La Blanche.

However, according to the prevalent AOC regulation, Calvados must be aged at least two years in oak casks, which gives it some tannin and color. In 2001, well ahead of Blanche d' Armagnac (AOC in 2005), and Cognac (2010 Rémy Martin for the USA) I decided to release the un-aged version of the spirit used to make Calvados Pays d'Auge and give up the Appellation d'Origine Contrôlée. We named it La

Blanche de Normandie and later La Blanche de Christian Drouin, therefore re-creating a category which had not been marketed for a long time.

Blanche flows out of the still, warm and colorless, to be stored in stainless steel vats for a minimum 12 months. It is as clear as vodka, but it does not intend to compete with vodka's neutrality. La Blanche does not have the complexity or character that old Calvados has, but it is surprisingly smooth, and delivers fresh and intense cider apple aromas. Ours was rated "highly recommended" by both the *Spirit Journal* (2006) and *Wine Enthusiast* (2007).

Thanks to bartenders, La Blanche, one of the most mixable spirits, has undergone a revival. It can also be appreciated neat, chilled, or over ice either as an aperitif or as an after-dinner drink.

During one of my trips to Russia, as I was introducing La Blanche to a Calvados party dinner as a cocktail ingredient, somebody stood up immediately and told me: "Stop! Here you are in Russia, we do not mix, we drink!" Since the Russian drink vodka with food, why not try La Blanche? New matches have been successfully explored: La Blanche enhances the flavor of smoked salmon and sturgeon, seafood, red caviar (or black if you can afford it), chorizo, zakouskis, and tapas. It also matches well with sushi and red tuna tartare, or even lemon pie during dessert. And what about a lime sherbet spiced up with fresh mint leaves and La Blanche?

La Pomme Prisonnière

La Pomme Prisonnière, as the name suggests, is a whole apple captured in a flask of Calvados. This is a venture I started in 1979 with the Alleaume family, fifth-generation apple-growers. I am proud of having been the first producer to use an apple rather than a pear.

Bottles are tied to the branches of an apple tree, and the apples grow inside the bottle. The harvest takes place in September and October. Unfortunately, it is very difficult to grow an apple in a bottle, much more difficult than growing a pear. The average rate of success is around 45%. The apple macerates in Calvados for one year. The skin of the apple delivers some bitterness and aromas while the apple juice brings in sweetness. The result is full-bodied Calvados with a very fruity character.

Another challenge was obtaining the necessary decisions from administrations such as whether to maintain the appellation Calvados Pays d'Auge, what volume of spirit (accounting for the liquid displaced by the apple) would be accepted, what quantity of alcohol would be taxed, and so on. Solving these questions was quite difficult and required a lot of patience.

"Pomme Prisonnière" was launched in 1981, and has enabled many consumers to discover Calvados. Puzzled by the captive fruit in a decanter full of spirit, many would

just ask: "How did you get the apple in?" When they get the answer, they are curious to taste the product inside the bottle. Funnily, Pomme Prisonnière helped me find my first agent in the United States: Stanley Stankiwcz, the late owner of Twelve Stone Flagons, who saw bottles of Pomme Prisonnière at Hédiard's in Paris and told a journalist that he was going to import the product. At that time, we had not met yet and he was totally unknown to me. So, I just happened to learn he intended to import our products through a British newspaper article.

Pommeau de Normandie

Pommeau de Normandie is a blend of freshly pressed apple juice and Calvados at a ratio of three to one, aged in wooden barrels for a minimum of 14 months. It must be bottled with alcohol content between 16% ABV and 18% ABV.

The length of aging in cask has a strong influence on its aromatic profile. Extra aging results in better balance with no apparent alcohol. Older pommeau develops a very complex nose with dry fruits flavors, rancio, and a deep, complex mouth. However, the regulation does not allow the producer to indicate any age on the label. It is less readily available outside France than Calvados, but one can find Pommeau de Normandie in the United States.

Made on Norman farms for centuries, pommeau could not be marketed because it was not regulated. It was not until 1986 that a regulation formalized the production and marketing of Pommeau de Normandie. The man behind this regulation is Edmond Chort-Mutel who challenged the French administration from 1948 to 1986. The decree defined pommeau process rules and guaranteed the typicality of this aperitif. In 1991, Pommeau de Normandie got its own AOC Appellation.

Its unique character and quality were immediately recognized. In 1986, I was the first producer to ship pommeau to the USA and Robert Parker was one of the very first Americans to taste it. He declared in *Wine Advocate*: "Never have I been so enchanted by a before dinner drink as this ...on the palate this aperitif is gorgeously fresh and quite fascinating to sip."

Pommeau de Normandie should be served chilled (46°F to 50°F) in a tulip or port glass. It is appreciated for its apple aromas, fruit exuberance, and natural moderate sweetness. Before dinner one can sip it neat or serve it in cocktails. It adds delicious apple perfume to many dishes, which can also be served with a glass of chilled pommeau.

Apple and Pear Gin

Apple gin, once used in cocktails as described in the *Café Royal Cocktail Book* (1937), was defined as gin combined with the soluble ingredients of the apple. Guillaume Drouin, now CEO of Calvados Christian Drouin, was a pioneer in re-creating this category of apple gin, which had not been produced commercially for a long time.

In November of 2015, he launched the first Norman apple gin incorporating a distillate of cider made from more than 30 varieties of cider apples and seven botanicals, calling it "un Gin de terroir." In 2023 he launched the first perry pear gin, Gin Pira, elected World Best Signature Botanical Gin at World Drinks Awards. Some other Calvados producers have followed in Normandy using different processes, releasing products such as "Gin Normindia" and "C'est Nous".

Other Products

In 1986, Georges Levêque created the first Crème de Calvados by blending Norman cream and Calvados at la Ferme du Loterot. Other producers have followed (Boulard, Busnel, Dupont, Huet, Laika, Lait douceur, Maitre Pierre, Nuage, etc). One can also find a number of Calvados based liqueurs. In 2024, Drouin launched ABC (Apéritif à Base de Calvados), which is an aperitif inspired by the vermouth category.

Scotch Whisky/Calvados Blend

In 2019, Scotch Whisky blender Compass Box released a new expression called Affinity, a spirit drink composed of Scotch whisky and Calvados, two complementary spirits. The Calvados was sourced from Christian Drouin distillery and blended with whiskies aged in French oak casks and Sherry butts. The blend includes malt whisky from Craigellachie alongside parcels of previously blended malts from Clynelish, Dailuaine and Teaninich distilleries.

Calvados in Cuisine

IN 2010, THE FRENCH GASTRONOMIC MEAL became part of UNESCO World Heritage. This is a feast meal meant to celebrate important moments in individuals and groups' lives. It gathers people who practice together the art of good food and good drinks. Starting with an aperitif and finishing with digestif, it is composed of four courses at a minimum: a first course, followed by fish and/or meat with vegetables, cheese and dessert.

There is no French gastronomic meal without digestif. By nature, Calvados is part of it. But young Calvados, due to its freshness and fruit flavor, also has aperitif virtues. Thus, it can be consumed as a pre-dinner or after dinner drink. It can even be served during the meal as "Trou Normand" or to match some dishes. It has also been part of many dishes' preparation ever since.

Calvados shows a remarkable span of styles and applications. It is one of the most versatile spirits in the world. From young and easy sipping to old and complex, Calvados can be enjoyed in many ways: some, such as digestifs and café Calva, are traditional. Others, such as in cocktails or with food pairings, have appeared more recently.

▶ **Traditional Calvados Moments**

The Legendary "Café Calva"

If you only drink American coffee in a large mug, skip this section!

One of the greatest calvados moments is the Café Calva, immortalized by great novelists like Erich Maria Remarque or Georges Simenon. Café Calva has enjoyed immense popularity in Norman farms and bistros since the 1880's.

This custom consists of pouring a little Calvados into your cup after finishing your coffee. The spirit warms up while gaining the coffee aroma and mingling with any sugar left in the cup. The flavor of the Calvados expand while the coffee becomes mellower.

The practice of Café Calva appeared in rural Normandy in the middle of the 19th century, then went on to conquer cities and their working-class suburbs. Men and women arriving from the Norman countryside to find work in the cities did not want to give up their Café Calva, which helped them put their hearts into their work despite arduous conditions. On the counters of Parisian bistros, "calva" was most often poured directly into coffee and, unless it was specified when ordering, coffee was systematically topped with Calvados.

A new consumption ritual was born, and it became a phenomenal success. The spirit's poor quality matched the coffee's bad quality, however, as consumers could not afford anything but cheap drinks. As a result, the image of Calvados was deeply damaged by this ritual created by and for hard-working classes. With rural depopulation, deindustrialization, and significant improvements in working conditions, Café Calva gradually disappeared from the bistro counters of country towns and the working-class suburbs of Northwestern France.

Today, however, Calvados has regained its legitimacy and the consumption of quality coffee has never been stronger. As a result, the Café Calva is experiencing a revival. Bars of Parisian palaces, fashionable cocktail bars, and fine restaurants are exploring the combination of coffee and Calvados with creativity. I, too, can recommend the association of coffee and Calvados, which is a real love marriage. Depending on the circumstances, you can savor an old Calvados in a tasting glass immediately after coffee, as the latter beautifully prepares your palate. Or, you can add a few drops of young Calvados to your ristretto or pour a little Calvados into the bottom of the empty, still hot cup of coffee. You can also rediscover this association in an after- dinner cocktail, such as a Calvados Espresso Martini or the Norman Coffee, a very gratifying wintertime recipe

NORMAN COFFEE

- 1 1/2 ounce Calvados
- 3 ounces strong, hot coffee
- 2-3 spoonfuls of simple syrup or cane syrup
- 1 ½ ounce light cream
- Cinnamon powder

Freeze the cream for 20 minutes before whipping it. Mix the simple syrup and Calvados and heat gently before pouring into a glass. Pour the hot coffee onto the mix very delicately to keep layers separate. Top with whipped cream, using the back of a coffee spoon to float the cream gently on top of the coffee and sprinkle with cinnamon

Le Trou Normand

> *"Between each course one made a hole, the Norman hole,*
> *with a glass of cider spirit which put fire to bodies and craziness to minds"*
> Guy de Maupassant, *Les Contes de la Bécasse,* 1883

Long ago, Norman people noticed the positive effects of a little glass of Calvados taken as a shot in the middle of a substantial meal cooked with butter and cream. This tradition of the Trou Normand, or "Norman hole," is intended to burn a hole in the stomach that will then make room for the rest of the courses. Thanks to the spirit, the stomach is freed all of a sudden of the food already absorbed, thus giving way to a renewed appetite. Choosing old Calvados for Trou Normand is useless, as it will not be savored as it should. Young Calvados is perfectly fine, and a half-ounce shot is plenty.

A true Trou Normand requires some solemnity. Guests should stand up, raise their glasses, and hold them in front of their faces. They should admire the color, breathe the Calvados in, and then drink it straight at the master of ceremony's command.

With the development of a lighter style of cuisine, the digestive qualities of Calvados that had been much appreciated by hearty eaters are less requested. The traditional Trou Normand is often replaced by apple granita topped with Calvados. But for Christmas or Thanksgiving dinner, this practice is highly recommended.

Digestif

Quality Calvados found its way onto the drinks trolleys of leading restaurants in the 1980s. Old and complex Calvados are to be reserved for after dinner tasting when the aroma and flavor can be appreciated at leisure.

Old Calvados develop an incredible palette of flavors. Ideally, Calvados should be served in a crystal tulip-shaped glass at room temperature. If the bottle is opened for the first time, it is important to let the volatile components disappear before pouring the Calvados. This does not take more than 5 minutes.

The ceremony may now begin: pour Calvados with care in your glass, warm it tenderly in the hollow of your hand, run it slowly round the glass (held by its base) and admire its color and the patterns it traces on the side of the glass. Calvados should be clear and the color should be nice, yet color and clarity do not give any information on the quality. It needs to breathe to develop its aromas — wait at least two minutes — before bringing the glass to your nose to find the distance at which you can distinguish the aromas without being assailed by the alcohol. It is recommended to put some drops under the tongue first to let the palate become accustomed to the alcohol strength. Savor your Calvados, sip by sip. You will note a surprising development in flavor and taste: from the lightest to the heaviest, aromas will develop for about one hour. Consumers expect to have a smooth Calvados, rich in aromatics and in persistence of flavor, full-bodied with a lingering finish.

The Trou Normand in Tokyo

With Cigars

Calvados and cigars are best friends, and old Calvados is especially appealing to cigar lovers. For the connoisseur, smoking a good cigar is a pleasure often associated with the drinking of brandy, whisky, or Port. However, the marriage of Calvados and cigar is one of the most perfect ones. In 1989, when a friend of mine considered one of Switzerland's foremost spirit authorities told me he was a close friend of Zino Davidoff, I asked him to give him a

How Long Does an Open Bottle Keep?

Quite often, I am asked how long you can keep a bottle once it is opened. The more air you have in the bottle, the more aromas you are going to lose. Keeping an opened bottle a few months, even one year, is no serious problem, but you gradually lose some of the aromas. So, my suggestion is to drink the content within six months to enjoy the best of it.

Finger Foods, photo © Yoshie Maruyama, Tokyo

bottle of my Calvados Pays d'Auge Hors d'Age to taste with cigars. Some time later, I received a handwritten letter from Davidoff dated April 3, 1989 concluding: "I've tried, it's wonderful!"

His judgment was confirmed by the French magazine *L'Amateur de Cigare* in its March 1996 issue following a tasting organized at The Ritz Hotel in Paris: "a fascinating mystery lies hidden in this spirit, one of the most subtle and complex produced on French soil, and probably the most naturally elegant," the magazine reported. "connoisseurs familiar with Calvados were pleasantly surprised by the quality of the palette of flavors and the delicacy of this spirit, which was even considered more jubilant than Cognac or Armagnac." Associations between Cigars and Calvados were described as "a marriage full of tenderness," "a voluptuous union," or "a handsome, well-matched couple."

For many years now, I have been invited by top Cigar Clubs throughout the world to conduct Calvados and cigar tastings. The association of cigar and Calvados was unanimously acknowledged to be a perfect alliance of flavors.

In Cuisine

> *"Calvados takes its name from the department of Calvados in Normandy. It is a fertile, green land of apple orchards and meadows, where apples, cream and of course Calvados feature strongly in the cooking... Calvados is a splendid brandy for cooking...My favorite Calvados recipes include escargots au calvados, foie gras frais de canard poêlé au calvados and, best of all, aumonières (crêpes) aux pommes."*
> —Michael Edwards, Caterer & Hotelkeeper, April 30, 1992

Calvados has been a long-time favorite ingredient of Norman chefs to add flair to fine cuisine. With globalization, Calvados is now appearing in other cuisines, where it adds depth to simple dishes.

Regarding quality, quite often one hears people say: "It doesn't matter, it's just for cooking." On the contrary: When using Calvados in cooking, you are meant to taste the apples and pears of Normandy. Thus it should be good quality, rather young and highly fruity. Concentration of apple aromas and lightness of tannin are essential to success. Young Calvados is the liveliest option: two to five years is the optimal age for cooking, but it must be carefully selected. Cheap Calvados will deliver alcohol rather than flavor and aroma.

There are three main ways to incorporate Calvados into a dish: flambéing, deglazing, or simply the direct addition as flavoring to a dish.

Flambé

The practice of flambéing is spectacular to look at, and adds a delicate flavor to the dish. A perfect complement to poultry or pork recipes, a Calvados flambé also enhances apple and pear desserts. Seafood such as shrimp or lobster will taste delicious if you broil them, flambé them, and then top them with melted butter. Blood pudding, a simple and cheap dish, will taste quite different and fancy when flambéed. Flambé a roast duck or pheasant to add apple-like aromas to the skin and flavor the gravy. To emphasize the Norman character of these aromas, just add baked apples and some fresh cream. As for flambé pancakes, they are world famous, as is flambéed tarte fine aux pommes (apple pie) or crème brûlée aux pommes.

Deglaze

Calvados is often used to deglaze a pan and add flavor to creamy sauces. Using Calvados to deglaze the frying pan in which veal cutlets have just cooked and then adding fresh cream is one of the classical ways of preparing Norman veal. Poulet Vallée d'Auge, another classic in French gastronomy, is also prepared by flambéing the chicken and then deglazing the pot with Calvados before adding double cream.

Direct addition

Calvados is often used to flavor pâtés, duck, or rabbit terrines. The combination of Calvados and fresh cream added to a sauce gives spectacular flavor to the dish. Adding some drops of Calvados to whipped cream used to top baked apples will make one splendid and simple dessert — and nothing can match Tarte Tatin better than Calvados ice cream.

All over the world, chefs enjoy cooking with Calvados. In the United States, I have had the opportunity to discover delicious recipes invented with Calvados, such as a chicken liver mousse flavored with apples and Calvados, and a simple salad dressing made with one part of balsamic vinegar, two parts of virgin olive oil and a teaspoon of Calvados. In Italy I was given the opportunity to taste some

Livarot, camermbert and Pont-L'Evêque, photo © Julien Boisard

interesting recipes such as millefeuilles of rocket salad and swordfish marinated in Calvados with stewed apples, risotto with cacciocavallo cheese and Calvados, and braised buffalo with Calvados. If you want to form your own opinion, I suggest you try one of the following recipes — or, even better, exercise your creativity by creating a personal recipe.

▶ Pairing Calvados and Food

Interest in the pairing of food and wines has developed considerably since the 1980s. Sommeliers have had remarkable success in finding associations between food and wines. Yet not all food can be successfully matched with wine: spicy dishes or food with a pronounced taste often kill its savor.

Sommeliers in countries with a developed wine culture such as France or Italy have traditionally shown a limited interest in spirits, even though they can sometimes be a better alternative. Conversely, drinking spirits during a meal is traditional in many countries with a spirits culture: Vodka in Russia or Poland for example, aquavit in Scandinavia, rakija in the Balkans, baiju in China, etc. With the decompartmentalization of the universe of bars and restaurants, the bartender now plays a role equivalent to that of the sommelier in a traditional restaurant. His knowledge in spirits enables him to propose perfect matches between food and spirits, whether neat or in cocktails — and Calvados offers an exceptional range of possibilities.

photo © Christian Drouin

Due to their higher alcohol content, straight spirits are harder to pair with food than cocktails are. This observation has given birth to the "foodtail," the alliance of food and cocktails. For several years now, we have also witnessed the development of the dinner aperitif as a meal on its own. Spirits now find their place here.

Chilled, La Blanche beautifully matches red caviar (eggs of salmon), oysters, herring, marinated or smoked salmon, antipasti del mare, and other raw or marinated fish dishes. I remember a meal organized in Calabria around Calvados attended by several great chefs from the region: A pairing of a raw tuna dish with La Blanche was unanimously recognized as the best possible association. A thin slice of Parma ham sublimates a well-balanced calvados, such as a VSOP. Other successful Italian marriages include eggplant Parmigiana or fritto misto di terra with Calvados Reserve, or zuppa di pesce with Calvados VSOP.

In Canada, I was given the opportunity to enjoy in the prestigious Montreal University Club the marriage of our Calvados Pays d'Auge XO with a North African lamb tajine. In Tokyo, I discovered in a Chinese restaurant that spicy Szechuan cuisine went remarkably well with Calvados Pays d'Auge VSOP, just like sweet and sour dishes do. Likewise, I also enjoyed a convincing experience offered by master chef Kouichirou Shimura at The Tempura Ono in Tokyo: a succession of tempura dishes paired with Calvados. Calvados cleans the palate of the savor of frying oil just as it goes with the fat of a soft-ripened cheese or with Middle Eastern pastry marked by oil and honey. Indeed, food cooking styles from all over the world offer numerous possibilities of marriage with Calvados and deserve to be explored.

With the comeback of raw and whole milk farmhouse cheeses with strong regional identity, pairing Calvados and cheese is also arousing growing interest, whether it be a cheese aperitif or a traditional service before dessert. A good meal in Normandy features great cheese from Pays d'Auge: Camembert, Pont- l' Evêque, and Livarot. The question often asked about such cheese coming from one of the few regions of France that does not produce wine is: "What should one serve?"

For Martine Nouet, an expert in food and spirits pairing, Calvados, depending on the kind of cheese, makes a perfect alliance. Pont-L'Evêque, with its creamy texture, enhances the fruitiness of Calvados Hors d'Âge. Calvados Domfrontais, lively and fruity, is the best match for Camembert, while Livarot, with its stronger flavor, goes very well with older Calvados and its overtones of spice and baked apples. Other associations with French cheeses are particularly interesting, such as extra-old Comté with Hors d'Age Calvados or Fourme d' Ambert with VSOP.

With the development of international trade, Calvados and cheese combinations are no longer limited to French cheese. They are becoming increasingly subtle: Thomas Girard, Head Bartender at Operation Dagger in Singapore, recommends pairing Calvados Pays d' Auge Christian Drouin finished in a Muscat de Rivesaltes cask with Stilton, the king of British cheeses. "It is able to stand up to this very expressive Stilton, highlighting its saline side. As for the alcohol, it breaks the fat of the cheese which softens its strength." One can make the same remark concerning the match between creamy Gorgonzola and soft, round-bodied aged Calvados Pays d'Auge. The 2015 world champion cheese-monger, Fabien Degoulet, considers Calvados VSOP a perfect match with Parmigiano Reggiano stravecchio. One can also consider matching Pecorino mezzo stagionato with Calvados Reserve.

As for dessert, Calvados is the perfect match for apple-based dishes, no matter how the apples are prepared. Old Calvados, with its beautiful pastry aromas, will wonderfully match crème brûlée, caramel sauce, filled crepes, apple or pear crumble topped with cream, or tarte tatin, in which the flavor of the apples is accentuated by the caramelization of the fruit. La Blanche, on the other hand, is the perfect top to lemon or lime sherbet. Old Calvados also goes wonderfully well with the flavors of bitter chocolate. A small glass of old Calvados with chocolate truffles flavored with Calvados is a most sensual and delightful experience.

Pommeau de Normandie also offers many possibilities of pairing. You may enjoy a glass of Pommeau with dishes such as smoked eel pâté, goose and duck foie gras toast with caramel, Stilton pie, pigeon tagine with dates, roasted guinea-fowl deglazed with Pommeau, banana gratin, duck breast roasted with honey, sweet potatoes with ginger syrup and dates, chocolate profiteroles, salty caramel and chocolate cake, or caramel and gingerbread mousse. You may also experiment with Pommeau-flavored custard, pear and chestnut pie, almond and Morello cherry cream, caramelized apple and whipped cream mille-feuilles. and many other dishes — just use your imagination.

▶ Calvados Recipes

CHICKEN LIVER MOUSSE

Calvados is used to flavor many pâtés as well as duck or rabbit terrines.

Serves 4 to 6

- ½ pound chicken livers
- ½ large onion or 1 smaller onion
- 2 Granny Smith apples
- 8 T or one stick cold unsalted butter, cut into small pieces
- 1 ½ oz. Calvados
- Salt and pepper, to taste
- Toast, for serving

Clean the chicken livers.

Slice the apples and onion thinly.

Cook the livers over low heat in a pan in very little butter. Make sure you do not overcook the livers which must remain rosy.

In another pan, cook the apples and onion until soft.

In a food processor, blend the chicken livers, apples, onion, salt, and pepper. Let cool in the bowl of the food processor. When cool, add the butter and Calvados and blend to a very smooth texture. Taste to check the seasoning. You may add some additional Calvados if needed. Chill for 2 or 3 hours. Serve in individual bowls with some toast.

SHRIMP SALAD WITH RED PEPPER, FLAMBÉED WITH CALVADOS

Deglazing a pan with Calvados is fast, dramatic, and adds a delicious flavor to the dish.

Serves 4

- 1 pound large shrimp
- 3 oz. Calvados
- 1 T whipping cream
- 1 oz. extra-virgin olive oil
- One pinch of red pepper powder
- Salt and pepper, to taste
- Lettuce
- French bread, for serving
- For the salad dressing:
- 2 T extra-virgin olive oil
- 1 T balsamic vinegar
- 1 tsp. Calvados
- Salt and pepper, to taste

To make the dressing, combine all ingredients in a small bowl.

Add the Calvados to a small saucepan and place over medium heat.

While the Calvados, heats, season the shrimp with red pepper, salt, and pepper. Heat the olive oil in a frying pan over medium-high heat. Add the shrimp, and cook for two minutes on each side.

Carefully use a long match or lighter to light the Calvados, then carefully pour the flaming liquid over the shrimp. Add cream and toss to combine.

Arrange the warm shrimp on a bed of lettuce. Dress with the salad dressing and serve with French bread.

SCALLOPS WITH POMMEAU-CARAMELIZED CHICORY

A tasty, unusual, and easy scallop recipe.

Serves 4

    16 large fresh scallops

    1 ½ pounds of Belgian endive, cut into ½ inch pieces

    3 oz. Pommeau de Normandie

    2 oz. butter

    Salt and pepper, to taste

Clean the scallops without letting them soak in water, then blot dry on paper towel.

Heat one ounce of butter in a nonstick pan over medium-low heat. Add the chicory and cook until tender, seasoning with salt and pepper to taste. Once tender, add the Pommeau and let the juice slowly reduce to caramelize the chicory.

In the meantime, heat another nonstick pan over medium-high heat. Add the butter, then cook the scallops for about one minute on each side, or until light brown. Do not overcook, and do not season the scallops.

Plate the Pommeau-caramelized chicory on a warm plate, and surround with the scallops.

VEAL CHOPS À LA NORMANDE

This is a traditional Norman recipe.

This recipe can also be made using other meats, such as pork.

Serves 4

    4 ⅓-inch-thick veal chops, seasoned with salt and pepper on each side

    4 oz. fresh cream

    2 tsp. calvados

    ½ pound mushrooms, cleaned and sliced

    2 oz. unsalted butter

    A pinch of fresh thyme

    2 oz. unsalted butter

    Salt and pepper, to taste

In a pan over medium heat, sauté the mushrooms in one ounce of butter, seasoning with salt and thyme, until tender and lightly browned.

Heat one ounce of butter in a hot frying pan. Add the veal chops, letting them brown slightly on each side. Then lower the heat and cook, flipping occasionally, for 6-8 minutes, or until cooked to desired doneness. Remove the meat to a warmed plate and deglaze the pan with Calvados. Return the veal chops to the pan and add the cream and mushroom mixture. Heat through and serve.

CINNAMON PANNA COTTA WITH "CALVAMELIZED" APPLE COMPOTE

This dessert is a Norman interpretation of the Italian classic.

Serves 4

    For the panna cotta

    1 cup heavy cream

    1 cup whole milk

    ¼ cup sugar

    1 cinnamon stick

    1 vanilla bean, split lengthwise

    1 packet plain unsweetened gelatin

    3 T cold water.

    For the apple compote:

    1 medium sized Granny Smith apple, peeled, cored, and diced into ½ inch pieces

2 T butter
2 T brown sugar
3 T calvados

To make panna cotta, combine cream, milk, cinnamon sticks and vanilla in a sauce pan. Bring to a simmer over medium heat and then remove from heat. Allow the spices to infuse for 30 minutes, then strain out spices.

In a small bowl, sprinkle gelatin on cold water. Let it soften for five minutes.

Heat the cream mixture again until it is very warm. Add the gelatin and stir until the gelatin is totally dissolved.

Divide the mixture into four small bowls and refrigerate for at least two hours, or until firm.

While the panna cotta chills, make the compote. Heat the butter in a frying pan over medium-high heat. Add the apple, sugar, and Calvados and cook, stirring frequently, until caramelized, five to 10 minutes. Allow to cool. Top the panna cotta with the "Calvamelized" apple compote.

CALVADOS FLAMBÉED TARTE

This classic of French cuisine is also called Tarte Fine.

Serves 8

For pâte sablée
7 oz. all-purpose flour
2 oz. granulated sugar
3 ½ oz. cold unsalted butter, cut into small pieces
1 egg yolk
2-3 T cold water
Pinch of salt

For the filling
2 pounds firm dessert apples, cored and peeled
2 oz. granulated sugar
4 oz. Calvados

To serve
Whipped cream, flavored with Calvados (optional)

To make the pâte sablée, add all ingredients to a food processor and pulse to blend. Do not overmix. Make sure the dough is neither too dry nor too damp. Flatten the dough into a disk, wrap in plastic wrap, and chill in the fridge for at least one hour.

Remove dough from refrigerator and roll out into a disk no thicker than 3/16ths of an inch. Place a tart pan with removable bottom on a baking sheet, and line with the dough.

Preheat oven to 350°F.

Prepare the filling. Cut the apples into wedges and arrange them in an attractive pattern on the dough disk. Sprinkle with sugar.

Cut the apples into thin wedges, arrange them nicely on the dough disk. Sprinkle with sugar. Bake the pie for 25 to 30 minutes, or until crust is browned and apples are tender.

Once the pie has been removed from the oven, heat the Calvados in a small pan over medium heat. Carefully set it alight, and then pour it over the tart. Serve with optional Calvados-infused whipped cream.

TARTE NORMANDE

This hearty dessert is a family classic.

Serves 6 to 8

For pâte brisée
1 cup all-purpose flour
A pinch of salt
A pinch of sugar
½ cup cold unsalted butter, cut into ½ inch pieces
4 T very cold water
One egg yolk (optional)

For the filling:
3 eggs
2 cups of dairy cream
½ ounce sugar
3 T Calvados
4 to 5 baking apples
A pinch of cinnamon

To make the pâte brisée, combine flour, salt, and sugar. Add the butter and cut in using a pastry blender. Once butter pieces are about the size of a pea, add the water one tablespoon at a time, gently blending with the pastry cutter. Adding an egg yolk to the pastry with the butter makes the dough more refined. Only add as much water as necessary for the dough to hold together when pressed. Do not overmix.

Gather the dough into a ball, flatten into a disk, sprinkle with flour, wrap in wax paper, and chill at least two hours before using.

Preheat oven to 350°F.

In the meantime, prepare the filling. In a medium bowl, whisk together eggs, cream, sugar, and Calvados. Peel and cut the apples into eight wedges of approximately equal size.

Roll out the dough into a circle about 3/16th of an inch thick. Line a flan ring or false-bottom tart pan with the dough. Arrange the apple wedges in an attractive pattern in the pastry shell, then pour the egg and cream mixture over the apples. Sprinkle with cinnamon, then bake for 45 minutes, or until the pastry is browned and the apples are tender. Serve warm.

APPLE SABAYON WITH CALVADOS

Serves 4

4 Granny Smith apples
Juice of one lemon
A pinch of cinnamon
1 T brown sugar
1 1/2 oz. butter
3 tbsp Calvados
3 to 4 oz. ginger cookies

For the sabayon
4 egg yolks
3 oz. sugar
6 oz. cider
3 T Calvados

Peel and cut each apple into 8 pieces and toss with lemon juice, sugar, and cinnamon.

Heat the butter in a pan over medium-high heat. Add the apple mixture and cook for a few minutes while you begin to heat the Calvados in a small pot over medium heat. Once warm, carefully light the Calvados on fire, then pour the flaming Calvados into the pan with the apples. Cook until the fire goes out, then remove from heat.

Chop the cookies into small pieces and divide the pieces evenly across four small baking dishes. Arrange the apples on top of the cookie crumbs.

In a small pot, whisk together sugar and egg yolks, then add cider and Calvados. Heat the mixture very gently over low heat (you can also use a double boiler), continually stirring until the mixture begins to thicken. Do not overcook, which could curdle the eggs.

Once the mixture is thick enough to coat the back of a spoon, pour it over the apples-crumb arrangement. Broil for a few minutes, or until the sabayon is lightly browned, and serve immediately.

CALVADOS CHOCOLATE TRUFFLES
This is a beloved Drouin family recipe.

- 8 oz. premium dark chocolate, roughly chopped
- 8 oz. extra fine unsalted butter, cut into small pieces
- 6 egg yolks
- 3 ½ oz. powdered sugar
- 2 ½ T Calvados
- 2 oz. unsweetened cocoa powder

In a double boiler, gently melt the chocolate. Once melted, remove from heat and allow to cool slightly.

In the meantime, combine the butter, egg yolks, sugar, and Calvados in a food processor. Process thoroughly until the mixture is whipped and fluffy. When the chocolate is just barely warm, blend it into the butter and egg yolk mixture.

Refrigerate the truffle mixture for a few hours, then use a teaspoon and your hands to form into 1-1.5 cm balls. Roll each ball in unsweetened cocoa powder and serve.

OMELETTE SOUFFLÉE WITH POMMEAU DE NORMANDIE
One bite of this dish, and you will understand the reputation of this Norman product.

Serves 2

- 3 eggs, whites and yolks separated
- 2 oz. granulated sugar
- 2 oz. Pommeau de Normandie
- 1 ½ oz. unsalted butter

Beat the egg yolks with the sugar and Pommeau until it makes a smooth cream.

Whip the egg whites to a soft peak.

Very delicately, fold the egg yolk mixture into the whipped egg whites.

Melt the butter in a hot frying pan, then pour the egg mixture into the pan. Let it cook for three minutes, then transfer the omelet to a dish and serve immediately.

CALVADOS AND POMMEAU SOUFFLÉ
Remember: guests may wait for a soufflé, but a soufflé should never wait for your guests!

Serves 6

- 2 oz. Pommeau de Normandie
- 3 oz. Calvados
- 6 egg yolks
- 12 egg whites

6 oz. caster sugar, plus more for dish.
1 oz. cornstarch
3 oz. whole milk
8 sponge biscuits
1 oz. butter

Preheat oven to 360°F.

Prepare a medium soufflé dish. Grease the interior generously with butter, then coat with about one ounce of granulated sugar, reserving any sugar that doesn't stick for the soufflé batter.

Place sponge biscuits in a baking dish or shallow pan. Combine Pommeau and Calvados, and pour over sponge biscuits to soak.

Add milk to a small pot and heat over medium heat until almost boiling.

While it heats, combine three ounces of the remaining sugar with the egg yolks, sugar, and cornstarch in a food processor. Beat until the mixture turns white, then add the hot milk and blend again.

Whip egg whites until stiff, adding the remaining sugar one spoonful at a time, beginning when egg whites reach the foamy stage.

Gently old the whipped egg whites into the egg yolk and milk mixture.

Pour about a quarter of the better in the soufflé dish. Add the soaked sponge biscuits. If any Calvados/Pommeau mixture remains in the dish, add it to the remaining egg and milk mixture. Pour the rest into the soufflé dish over the sponge biscuits. The dish should not be more than ¾ full.

Bake for 20 to 25 minutes. Do not open the oven door during cooking. Once the soufflé has risen and begun to brown, transfer immediately from oven to table.

Other Pommeau de Normandie cooking ideas:

- Pour Pommeau de Normandie into the center of a seeded cantaloupe half
- Marinate duck foie gras in Pommeau for an hour before baking it
- Bake scallops in cream sauce flavored with shallots and Pommeau
- Stuff quails with raisins macerated in Pommeau before baking them in butter
- Flavor tarte tatin with Pommeau caramel and top with fresh cream
- Inspired by a dish offered in Segafredo Japan coffee shops, top vanilla ice cream with Pommeau de Normandie — a lovely match for the easiest of all deserts

Marc Jean, photo © Julien Booisard

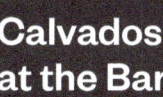

Calvados at the Bar

CALVADOS IS NOT ONLY FOR drinking straight. Calvados and applejack are also closely bound up with the history of cocktails, and they have experienced times of glory and obscurity behind the bar.

▶ The Early Years

According to historians, the word *cocktail* appears for the first time in 1806 in an American magazine to designate a drink made of one spirit, sugar, water, and bitters — that is to say, an Old Fashioned. The recipe does not specify the nature of the spirit but there is almost no doubt that apple brandy, the first spirit to be made in the United States, was the base of an old fashioned in the early 1800s.

▶ The Golden Age

The golden age of cocktails in America developed in the second half of the 1800s and ended with Prohibition. It was characterized by perfectly made cocktails with meticulous details — often short, highly alcoholic, and created by legendary bartenders. The use of splits and fruit juices was minimal. The first bartender's guide written by an American, *The Bartenders Guide: How to Mix Drinks, or The Bon Vivant's Companion,* by Jerry Thomas, was published in 1862. It marked the start of an incredibly creative period in cocktails and cocktail books.

Prohibition in the United States from 1920 to 1933 played a key role in propagating cocktail culture in other countries. When drinking alcohol became illegal, customers flocked to "speakeasy" bars, hidden away in the most unlikely places, to drink largely adulterated products that were only palatable mixed in cocktails. To be able to enjoy good spirits, American consumers had to leave the United States.

Wealthy Americans boarded cruise boats where they could savor quality products in international waters. Many travelled to Europe on legendary ocean liners like the

French "Normandie." As barmen could no longer practice their trade in the United States, they immigrated to other countries — in particular Great Britain and France —contributing to the development of cocktails and the expansion of American bars. In Europe, Calvados successfully replaced applejack in recipes and became one of bartenders' favorite basic alcohols.

Paris was a preferred destination. It had become the world capital. All those who were inventing modern art were to be met there: Picasso, Apollinaire, Modigliani, Max Jacob, Aragon, Soutine, Man Ray, Braque, Matisse, Breton, Fujita, Van Dongen, Gertrude Stein, Scott Fitzgerald, Hemingway, Sydney Bechet, Django Reinhardt, Josephine Baker, and many others. They were painters, poets, writers, sculptors, musicians, merrymakers, and lovers. They were free. Champagne, wine, and spirits flowed. Calvados was not to be forgotten: when in Paris, Ernest Hemingway always carried a silver flask with "From Mary, with love" engraved in which he carried excellent old Calvados. After the war, as an antidote to fits of the blues, he asked for the help of Calvados, "this faithful old servant".

When Paris became a major cocktail scene during the "Roaring Twenties," Normandy — the gateway to Great Britain and the United States — also tuned into the cocktail hours. Even before World War I, Le Havre had a well-known bar at Hotel Frascati where one could meet celebrities of the time, including the legendary Sarah Bernhardt. Deauville, most glamorous resort of the Norman coast, with its casino, its palaces and its foreign and Parisian clientele, soon became a well-known cocktail center. T. Van Dyke at Ciro's bar in Deauville created the Block and Fall cocktail in 1924, with a split base that put Calvados and Cognac on equal footing. It inspired the Deauville cocktail, which dates back to 1930 and originated in New Orleans. It consisted of Calvados, brandy, triple sec, and fresh lemon juice in equal parts).

Throughout this golden age, Calvados was the base of many recipes published in bar & cocktail books. *Harry's ABC of Mixing Cocktails* by Harry MacElhone, with new material by Andrew MacElhone, proposed 14 Calvados-based recipes. *Café Royal Cocktail Book*, published in 1937 by the United Kingdom Bartenders Guild and compiled by William Tarling, gives more than 44 Calvados-based recipes. *The Savoy Cocktail Book* published in 1930 presents 49 Calvados cocktails, showing just how usual it was to use Calvados in cocktails in those days.

▶ **The Dark Era**

Prohibition and World War II rationing created a shortage of aged spirits, which was even more pronounced for Calvados due to German occupation and the battle of Normandy in 1944. In response, bartenders turned to neutral spirits requiring no aging but delivering no flavor: Vodka, which must be odorless and colorless, encountered unbelievable success. In doing so, bartenders gave up sophisticated cocktails and moved to mixed drinks that in fact were mere fruit juice with alcohol for the effect. Cocktails grew to fishbowl proportions and alcohol became the minor ingredient. They were appreciated for refreshment — even though a large drink served straight up gets warm before it is half-finished!

In the 1970s, as interest in cocktails continued to fade out, only bars of Grand hotels kept the tradition of classic recipes alive, without much creativity. Most bartenders lost their interest in brown spirits like Calvados, which were perceived as difficult to marry with other flavors due to the richness of their aromas and their intensity. Instead, bartenders gravitated towards white and neutral spirits. The king of them all was vodka, almost a non-entity during the golden era but poised to conquer the drinks world of the mid-20th century. Large companies able to produce millions of cases quickly became dominant on the spirit market. They greatly influenced the bartending community by pushing products that were easy to produce in volume and at low cost. What was a cocktail in the '70s? Vodka-based, weak, sweet and fruity.

During this time, most bartenders neglected Calvados and wonderful Calvados-based recipes created in the Golden Age fell out of fashion. Moreover, purchasers at grand hotels often replaced bartenders in deciding what products would be available in all bars — and, consequently, what cocktails could be created. If they were to use Calvados, the choice was a cheap and neutral one, adhering to the philosophy that "If it is to be mixed, quality doesn't matter."

Calvados producers of the time stayed away from the world of bars, considering their product too noble to be mixed and best reserved for traditional enjoyment. Cocktails were thoroughly out of fashion by the '80s, and Calvados almost disappeared from the cocktail menus. In 1985 when I asked to meet Daniel Willems, chief bartender at the Concorde Lafayette Hotel in Paris and President of the Association des Barmen de France, he stared at me for a long while and then uttered: "You are the first Calvados producer that has ever come and visited me, I was curious to see what a Calvados producer looked like!" But considering Calvados mixes very well in a variety of cocktails, I fully disagreed with my colleagues.

Starting in 1987, Jean-Paul Thomine, chief Bartender at Deauville Casino and President of Association des Barmen de France — Normandy (ABF Normandy) and I put our energy into reviving professionals' interest in Calvados by asking various associations who were International Bartender Association (IBA) members to create cocktails for books to be published by the Norman publisher Charles Corlet. New recipes created all around the world were published in four recipe books.

In 1990 I received an interesting letter from John Poister, the author of *The New American Bartender's Guide*. In it, he wrote: "Let me say that I am a great lover of Calvados, and my reluctance to use it in cocktails and other mixed drinks is the high cost of Calvados in New York. I find myself, when making the famous Jack Rose cocktail, using our own apple brandy, called popularly "Apple Jack". Allow me to hasten to add that Calvados in a superior product and I believe that a means can be found to attract more American drinkers to Calvados in some creative ways."

Commenting on the book I published with Jean-Paul Thomine, *Cocktails from Normandy*, he added: "Your drink recipes are imaginative and appealing and when my book is up for revision, I will include some of your drink recipes." A new cycle in cocktail history was in the making. It would offer much more favorable prospects for Calvados.

In the '90s, Calvados faced a totally new situation with growing interest in quality products, craft spirits, terroir, new export markets, and the nascent cocktail revival.

Clement Emery of Bar Le Botaniste, photo© Pierre Lucet-Penato

Faced with the stagnation of after-dinner drinks and considering the opportunities posed by the cocktail resurgence, Calvados producers eventually realized the advantages of promoting Calvados as a cocktail ingredient. These developments resulted in the Calvados producers' association (IDAC)' decision in 1996 to cooperate closely with ABF Normandy in running a highly professional competition: Calvados New Wave International Trophies. Jean-Paul Thomine and the whole team of ABF Normandy played a key role in building "Les Trophées" du Calvados. Despite such considerable efforts and the fact that Calvados is an ideal mixer, the list of IBA Official Cocktails still shows only one Calvados cocktail: the Angel Face, while French Bartenders who publish a separate list give only two: Jack Rose and Mojidos, a Calvados mojito.

▶ The Cocktail Revival and the Calvados Cocktail Renaissance

The craft cocktail movement is the origin of the current Calvados renaissance. It is characterized by the revival of traditional recipes and methods and the use of super-premium spirits. The star of the cocktail is the spirit at its base and the creation of the cocktail is organized around that spirit with the goal of delivering aromatic complexity, character, body, and length. No wonder Calvados, so long out of the limelight, made its comeback at the turn of the millennium.

One element of the cocktail revival is approachability. It acknowledged that people could feel intimidated by the atmosphere and prices at grand hotel bars. Instead, modern bartenders aimed to offer quality at affordable prices in a relaxed atmosphere. They raised the quality of their drinks with carefully selected fresh ingredients such as fresh fruit squeezed daily as well as fresh vegetables. Infusions, homemade syrups, or even homemade spirits. Smaller cocktails in dainty glassware provide the opportunity to use much higher quality liquors and to offer them at affordable prices. Consumers are responding to these new experiments, different and unusual drinks that have quality, heritage, a story, and include spirits with more flavor.

Today, most of the best bars around the world offer Calvados cocktails. They may be historical or revisited, bespoke cocktails, signature cocktails, or original drinks that express their creator's taste and personality. Curious to understand why top bartenders turned to Calvados for their cocktails, Guillaume Drouin and Alex Mermillod, export manager at Christian Drouin and a cocktail specialist, recently asked some of them in Paris. Here are their answers:

"As it is a fruity product, it is very easy to adapt to customer demand and to offer a tailor-made cocktail."
—Matthew Long

"Calvados greatly inspires me as I find it has true complexity and richness."
— Clement Emery

"It is the noblest of the fruity spirits…It is a highly versatile product that is particularly easy to work in a cocktail. It goes well with syrups, aperitifs, and mixes extremely well with vinous bases, be they dry or lemony."
—Margot Lecarpentier

"Apples bring matter, richness, crunchiness, and spicy notes."
— Raphaël Blanc

"Calvados is an intense spirit with fresh fruit that I appreciate."
— Diane Vandenbrooke

I like to steer a customer towards a category of spirit he doesn't know very well, like Calvados, by means of cocktail that is readily accessible."
— Louis Lebaillif

"Calvados has now become indispensable; a number of bars propose Calvados in their menus with diversified ranges, particularly with the advent of Les Blanches."
— Maxime Potfer

"Calvados is dear to my heart. It is not only one of the richest French spirits but also represents the Normandy terroir and the history of France."
— Christina Hernandez

"I am proud to have Calvados on the menu, which entails the use of no, or few, pesticides."
— Riccardo Merini

"When I discovered the world of Calvados, I fell in love with it.
— Aris Makris

The modern cocktail revival is more than a revival of the golden age. Mixology has moved cocktails beyond their traditional codes. Numerous trends keep surging concerning ingredients, methods, techniques, settings, flair bartending, and pairing cocktails with finger food and dishes. Molecular techniques are sometimes put forward while, at the same time, classic ingredients are adapted to modernize drinks drinks. Spirits such as soju, baiju, pisco, Tequila, and mezcal are becoming popular bases for cocktails alongside Calvados. Some cocktail bars focus on a single spirit, sometimes Calvados, such as Bar Calvador in Kyoto which offers more than 400 different Calvados. Coupette in London also has a focus on French spirits with a specialty on Calvados.

Whether classic, "speak-easy," or contemporary, cocktail bars are quickly increasing in numbers all over the world. Every large city has a cocktail scene, and traditional boundaries between types of establishments are breaking. Everywhere one can notice a blossoming of new culinary ideas due to the relationships between restaurants, cocktail bars, and even wine bars. Chefs, sommeliers and mixologists are exchanging ideas — and, as a result, mixologists' cocktails are beginning to look more and more like recipes for foods. Likewise, some sommeliers now suggest matches between food and spirits or food and cocktails.

Bartenders now form a global community, tied together by old and well-established recipes yet at the same time eager to innovate. They travel to attend huge international fairs such as Tales of the Cocktail, London Cocktail Week, Bar Convent Berlin, and other vibrant celebrations of an international cocktail scene. They also keep in touch via the internet and social media, allowing them instant access information from all over the world. This new environment creates new opportunities for smaller spirits categories — categories like Calvados — that have lacked the financial means to promote their products through expensive campaigns.

▶ Cocktails Scenes Around the World

Today, most major cities all over the world have their own cocktail scene. Four major historical scenes, however, are driving forces behind modern trends.

London

According to Simon Difford, author and the creator of Difford's Guide, the modern cocktail renewal does not originate in the U.S., but instead surged in London in the mid-'90s and then appeared in New York in the late '90s. "London is to cocktails what Paris is to gastronomy," asserts Bertrand Guillou-Valenin, chief bartender at the London Buddha Bar. Audrey Saunders, who started the Pegu Club in New York, described London to the New York Times as "the best cocktail city in the world."

London is the birthplace of many classics. Five-star hotel bars still dominate London's cocktail scene: The American bar at the Savoy, The Bar at the Dorchester, The Artesian at The Langham, The Library Bar at the Lanesborough Hotel, The Connaught Hotel Bar, the Dandelyan at the Mondrian, The Rivoli Bar at the Ritz, and The Punch Room at The London Edition are among the best cocktail bars in the world. They use quality products combined with expert execution and presentation. High priced, they are the private ground of a wealthy elite.

Apart from top hotel bars, however, London was not known as a flamboyant cocktail scene in the 1980s. Then came Dick Bradsell, considered the father of the cocktail revival that took root in London in the 1990s. He shook up the classics and served them up with a twist of modernity. "Everywhere he went, Bradsell instilled a range of bartending rules whose legacy is still felt today. Fruit juice had to be squeezed fresh, he believed in glasses chilled, ice used in copious quantities and hospitality joyfully enforced," wrote The Sipsmith Blog. A number of Bradsell's creations became modern classics, and he was a mentor to a number of today's leading bartenders, including Tony Conigliaro. According to Conigliaro, "The whole London scene has changed enormously: Consumers are much more knowledgeable, drinks have become much better and there is a pride in the crafting of cocktails that wasn't there before."

In the modern London cocktail scene, Calvados is widely recognized as a great spirit base for cocktails. In his book *365 Days of Cocktails: The Perfect Cocktail for Every Day of the Year*, Difford gives 13 Calvados-based cocktail recipes, including "The Last Straw," created in 2006; "Serendipity," referring to a Persian fairy tale, *The Three Princes of Serendip*, "The Velvet Threesome" in homage to rock icon Lou Reed, "The Steep Flight" to laud rocketman Roadman Law, one of the 20th century's unsung heroes; "Parisian Spring Punch" in honor of La Tour Eiffel; "Royal Smile" and "Blue Mountain Cocktail," both original creations of Difford, and classics including "The Widow's Kiss," the "Jack Collins," Harry Craddock's cocktail "The Star," and Charles Schumann's creation "Fallen Leaves."

Another British guru in Europe and the USA, Michael Jackson, was appreciative of Calvados: "One of the world's great brandies, the finest of apple distillates," he said. While visiting me at home after a Paris Whisky Live event, he agreed to taste a few samples of Calvados in the evening and have some more the next day because he was extremely tired. After tasting the first ones, he was so excited that he went on. When he went to bed the birds were already chirping. In his *Bar & Cocktail Book*, Jackson gives 13 Calvados-based cocktail recipes.

New York

In the early 1990s, New York's cocktail scene was dominated by vodka and London Dry Gin. According to Audrey Saunders of Pegu Club, "most people were experiencing sweet, fruity, flaccid mediocrity in a glass." The bar world was ruled by flashiness, noise, and carelessly done drinks.

An early pioneer of cocktail culture revival in New York and across the United States was Sasha Petraske (1973-2015), who opened his first bar, Milk & Honey, in 1999. It was a place of convivial civility, a bar where the entrance was hidden, the drinks classically rooted, the ingredients fresh, and the bartenders knowledgeable guides. He went on to be a partner and creative force behind many of the world's most highly regarded bars, and launched countless imitators. The model was so successful that it has become difficult for anyone to try something totally new.

Audrey Saunders

Another speakeasy-style bar offering mainly classic cocktails, Angel's Share, opened in 2004 and contributed greatly to New York 's resurgent cocktail culture. The owner wanted to create a Tokyo-style bar.

The roots of the cocktail revival in New York can also be traced back to Saunders, schooled under Dale De Groff at the Blackbird. At Pegu Club, which opened in 2006, she made a point of emphasizing quality technique over gimmickry. Many leading bartenders began their career at Milk & Honey or Pegu Club. One of them, Kenta Goto, spent seven years working closely with Sanders before opening Bar Goto, a Japanese-style bar that has become one of the top bars in New York.

Among all those who are behind the cocktail revival, Sean Muldoon and Jack McGarry also deserve a very special mention. Born in the same neighborhood in Belfast, they became two of the most prominent bartenders in the world, building a bridge between Great Britain and New York. Their venture started at Belfast's Merchant Hotel where they won number of international awards, including World's Best Cocktail Bar. Then they moved to New York, where they opened the Dead Rabbit in downtown Manhattan in 2013. It named the World's Best Bar in 2016. In 2022 they parted ways, with McGarry continuing to lead The Dead Rabbit.

Bar Goto in NYC, photo© Virginia Miller, theperfectspotsf.com

New York today is the neo-speakeasy capital of the world and one of the world's best craft cocktail bar scenes. All high-end cocktail bars offer comfort, gracious service, high quality, and fresh-made products, but often serve the same cocktails with different names, all pretty time-honored combinations of ingredients. A return to brown spirits, as well as the popularity of craft and classic cocktails, has favored the comeback of apple brandies, Calvados, and applejack in American cocktails. Most cocktail bars have at least one Calvados-based cocktail on rotation, and the trend has spread over all the United States. Every major American city has become a vibrant and creative cocktail scene promoting apple brandy and Calvados.

Leading writers across the U.S. have proclaimed the cocktail renaissance over since 2017. The popularity of craft cocktails has created more and more demand for cocktail programs. Craftsmanship has now given way to cocktail industrialization, and managers replace creative artists. Will high-quality ingredients, techniques, and liquors keep their place in an expanded scene? Or will the return of mediocrity bring a new dark era back? Let us hope quality will survive in a diversified American cocktail scene.

France

Until the beginning of the 2000s, cocktails in France were offered mostly at the bars of palace hotels and Calvados was not the star of the menus. There were a few exceptions, like the Hemingway bar at the Ritz Hotel in Paris where Chief bartender Colin Field had a personal interest in Calvados, calling it "the most beautiful, underrated alcohol in France." He created a few Calvados-based cocktails and one of them, Le Serendipity (his favorite cocktail), is now recognized as a French classic.

Most Palace hotel bars like Le Bar du Bristol, "Le Botaniste Bar at the Shangri La, Le 228 at Meurice Hotel, and Le Bar Kleber at the Peninsula now offer Calvados cocktails on a regular basis.

Recently, Paris has become one of the trendiest cocktail scenes. The rise of the craft bar movement started in 2007 with the opening of l'Expérimental Cocktail Club, a Parisian speakeasy created by Romée de Goriainoff, Pierre Charles Cros, and Olivier Bon. Many great bars have popped up in Paris during the last years, such as Classique Café, Combat,

Mesures, Castor Club, Divine, Boubalé, Kapara, and Cambridge Public House, as well as in Lyon (Sauvage), or Bordeaux (Symbiose). Cocktails are also now spreading into restaurants, from bistros to Michelin star restaurants.

In this very dynamic industry, French spirits are currently enjoying a new lease on life thanks to cocktails. One of the developments of the French cocktail scene is the return of products sourced closer to home. There are no great cocktails without quality ingredients. France owns a splendid list of flavors and traditional products which bartenders are now making their own: Armagnac, Calvados, Cognac, Pernod, Absinthe, Bénédictine, Chartreuse, Cointreau, Grand Marnier, Pineau des Charentes, Pommeau de Normandie, Lillet, Suze, Picon, Byrrh, and so forth.

Japan

I have visited Japan regularly since 1986 and noticed the permanence of a very high level of quality. Apart from the rest of the world, the Japanese cocktail scene has remained unique. However, American cocktail culture and Japanese cocktail culture heavily influenced each other over the 20th century, and the two retain an interdependent relationship.

Japanese cocktail culture dates back to the Meiji Period (1852-1912), when the country sent out ambassadors to bring home the best of other cultures. The first bar to serve cocktails opened in Yokohama's International Hotel in 1874 serving expatriates and occasionally local customers. Many Japanese bartenders learned western mixology abroad by working on ocean liners. This nascent cocktail culture may have been strengthened with the arrival of American bartenders in Japane after losing their jobs during Prohibition. If the first Japanese cocktails were expressions of American culture, Japanese bartenders quickly developed their own cocktail culture, which seems to be inspired by the ancestral tea ceremony and the inclusion of some Asian products, such as sake.

What exactly sets Japanese cocktail culture apart? A few years ago, I was doing a Calvados master class for a bartender's association in Tokyo. A young woman, a bar teacher, prepared a Calvados-based cocktail for the tasting. I was fascinated by how beautifully she was moving the spoon with effortless grace and elegance. I told her how amazed I was watching her prepare the cocktail. She confessed she had spent more than 2,000 hours learning how to move the spoon, practicing for so long that her fingers sometimes bled. Ice is another Japanese obsession: it must be crystal clear and perfectly hand cut. According to Kayama, owner of Ben Fiddich, "Japanese bartending technique" is not simply about using local ingredients; it is about connecting movements with elegance.

Japanese bartenders now take inspiration from all over the world, including Normandy. Because of their enthusiasm in promoting Calvados in Japan, two famous bartenders, Hiroyuki Takayama at Bar Calvador in Kyoto and Tomoaki Wasai at Bar Stag in Kitakyushu, Fukuoka, have officially been appointed Calvados Ambassadors by IDAC.

The Japanese way to prepare cocktails is a stylish ritual. Bartenders are usually dressed in immaculately white jackets. The service is unparalleled. The guest may order a cocktail from the menu, either a classic or a signature one, or the bartender may provide a more customized drink to an individual's taste. The guest might have to answer a few questions about his drink preferences. The ritual is carried out in front of him. The bartender lays out all of their tools and ingredients before starting. Their gestures are precise and beautiful, not theatrical.

Bartenders move subtly and quietly. They have spent years perfecting skills like

Bar Calvador, photo courtesy Virginia Miller, theperfectspotsf.com

cleaning, measuring, pouring, ice carving, stirring, and shaking. They strive for perfection through relentless practice, repetition and extreme attention to detail and use quality ingredients. Smooth and perfectly balanced cocktails are preferred to those with higher levels of alcohol, pastel shades are preferred to sharp vivid colors, and cocktails are served in dainty glassware.

Tokyo's drinking scene now welcomes boundary-breaking cocktail bars. They do not try to recreate a speakeasy, but instead integrate mixology culture in the most professional way. The best example I saw in Tokyo was Bar Ben Fiddich owned by Hiroyasu Kayama, which is a true temple of Japanese mixology. Going into this Shinjuku bar, not easy to find, makes you feel as if you are entering an alchemy temple from the Middle Ages: You are greeted by darkness, an old painting of an alchemist on the wall, antique liquor bottles, all kinds of infusions and homemade distillates, a huge collection of glasses, fresh fruit and vegetables, and a mysterious atmosphere.

In 2008, the American magazine *Bon Appétit* declared Tokyo the "cocktail capital of the world". Mixology is constantly changing and it is difficult to say which city is the cocktail capital of the world, but it is clear Japanese bartending greatly influences bartenders in the rest of the world.

▶ Choosing the Right Calvados for Cocktails

Calvados is the base for some of the oldest and best cocktails. Recently, mixologists have considerably extended the repertoire of Calvados cocktails. The current cocktail trend has given a new lease of life to the spirit from Normandy.

There is no great cocktail without quality ingredients. Calvados is a unique spirit combining fruit aromas and the aromatic notes delivered by barrel aging. It mixes better in cocktails than other cider-based spirits, delivering more apple flavor and adding a touch of elegance to the drink. Bartenders may tweak aromas in a spirit-based cocktail in the same way as a chef uses spices to bring out new flavors in a dish, but Calvados must be easily recognized.

It is crucial to choose Calvados with care. Calvados showing defects such as high concentrations of ethyl acetate giving aggressive, nail polish-like aromas, or tailsy Calvados with soapy, sulfurous notes should be avoided. Fortunately, such defects are most unlikely to be found in Calvados available on the market today. Commercial Calvados produced with added sugar, wood extracts, and artificial color should also be avoided. They deliver alcohol, sweetness, and rustic tannins rather than true fruit aromas and genuine aromas extracted from the barrel.

Different types of Calvados can serve different roles in a cocktail. If you are seeking fresh apple aromas with no tannins or color, La Blanche is ideal. Provided it is perfectly distilled and kept some time in a neutral tank, it will offer the necessary suppleness.

Calvados Pays d'Auge aged from 2 to 5 years (marked as Réserve or VSOP) is the ideal spirit for cocktails requiring aromatic complexity, body, and length. Calvados Domfrontais, which is distinguished by its exuberant fruity aromas, is suitable for cocktails calling for a fruit-based alcohol. Since the AOC Domfrontais requires over three years of aging in oak casks, some Calvados produced in Domfrontais which do not comply with the minimum aging are offered as Calvados AOC. Such is the case of Calvados Christian Drouin AOC Selection, which is acclaimed by many mixologists.

Because the Calvados AOC category is not as homogeneous as Pays d'Auge or Domfrontais, the bartender should specify the brand for accurate replication of its character.

In most cases, older Calvados of good origin will be perfect savored on its own in a glass, as it may be too wood-forward for a cocktail. Barrel aging enhances a spirit's body and taste as well as adding color. Yet in some recipes, Calvados Hors d'Age can contribute to great cocktails, provided the additional astringency from the oak tannins and spicy flavors be in balance with caramelized apple. When it comes to older Calvados, the simpler the cocktail, the better — such as an Old Fashioned.

Eric Felten, a columnist at the *Wall Street Journal*, wrote that "Purists will object to using a very old Calvados such as the Drouin Hors d'Age in any sort of cocktail. But a drink such as the Widow's Kiss can be adjusted to make the most of an elegant base spirit. Instead of 1.5 ounces Calvados to 0.5 ounce each of Chartreuse and Bénédictine, try 2 ounces of the apple brandy to a scant teaspoon each of the liqueurs for a refined Widow."

▶ Cocktail Recipes

In this section I present some emblematic Calvados-based recipes for inspiration. A majority of grand hotel bartenders follow the rules set by International Bartender Association (IBA) that were created in 1951 and established a list of classic cocktails that every member is supposed to know. The French are an exception, with a slightly different list of classic cocktails and some different rules, such as the use of only one base spirit, no more than six ingredients, no more than 7cl alcohol (2 1/3 ounces), and ingredients measured in cl or in tenths. In some countries measures may be in ounces or milliliters.

Modern bartenders have considerably extended and renewed the repertoire, choosing to free themselves from IBA rules. Most of their recipes are not aimed to be repeated. Although signature drinks are not new, they have recently become increasingly popular. A signature cocktail is an original drink that expresses the nature of the person or establishment creating it. It may designed to represent a theme or a color, often incorporating local ingredients and culture. At wedding receptions or at any special event, a signature cocktail can replace the entire offer of drinks.

In cocktails made with more than one spirit, Calvados mixes well with gin or Cognac. Combining Calvados with orange liqueur (triple sec, Cointreau, Grand Marnier, or Campari) always works. It also gives good results with most fortified wines, dry and sweet vermouth, most fruit juices (orange, apple, passion fruit, grapefruit), and does particularly well with lime or lemon juice.

Quite often, the simpler the cocktail the better. Calvados excels in old fashioneds, sours, gimlets, negronis, and spritzes.

▶ Historic Classics

It seems that before World War II, consumers ate and drank impressive quantities. Looking at the menus, we can wonder how it was possible to eat so much! As for historical cocktail recipes, the total quantities of alcohol contained in a cocktail are just amazing. Contemporary bartenders typically reduce significantly the quantity given in the original recipe while maintaining the proportions.

Some of the best Calvados-based cocktails came out between the 1860s and Prohibition. Some never disappeared, while lost and forgotten recipes are being discovered again. Classic cocktails are those that have stood the test of time. Flavor, balance, and complexity are achieved through the simplest combination of ingredients. A number of bartenders make cocktails the way they were made when they were first created, while others revisit them.

CALVADOS OLD FASHIONED
Dating back to 18092, the old fashioned is the oldest written cocktail recipe: spirit, sugar, and bitters. As America's oldest spirit, apple brandy was likely used to make those original old fashioneds.

This gloriously autumnal old fashioned variation was given to me by Jason Wilson. It wonderfully showcases Calvados, especially a younger bottling such as Christian Drouin Selection.

- 1 teaspoon pure maple syrup
- 2 dashes aromatic bitters
- 2 ounces Calvados
- 2 or 3 ice cubes

Combine the maple syrup and bitters in an old-fashioned glass. Add a third of the Calvados along with one ice cube, and stir gently for 20 seconds. Add another third of the Calvados and another ice cube and continue stirring gently for another 20 seconds. Add the rest of the Calvados, and one more ice cube if desired, while continuing to stir for another 20 seconds.

JACK ROSE

The Jack Rose is the only Calvados-based cocktail recipe figuring in Carnet de Cocktails Contemporains, *the official French list of classic cocktails. Originally, the Jack Rose was a sour made from applejack with grenadine as the sweetener. Some bartenders think that applejack is not optional in a Jack Rose, while others think that Calvados works better. Jack Rose recipes vary widely in strength, sweetness and the use of lemon or lime. The best one I have ever tasted was made from La Blanche and fresh lime juice in Singapore!*

Harry's ABC of mixing cocktails gives the following recipe for a Jack Rose:

- 2 ounces Calvados
- Juice of one lemon (I recommend freshly pressed juice)
- 4 dashes of grenadine (I recommend genuine pomegranate-based grenadine)
- Lemon wedge, for garnish

Combine all ingredients in an ice-filled shaker, shake, and strain into a chilled cocktail glass. Garnish with a lemon wedge.

One and a half ounces of Calvados, ¾ of an ounce of fresh lemon or like juice, and three dashes of pomegranate grenadine will give a drink of more modern proportions.

ANGEL FACE

This cocktail first appeared in the Savoy Cocktail Book *compiled by top New York bartender Harry Craddock and published in 1930.*

The Angel Face is the only Calvados-based cocktail in the official list of the International Bartender Association. Here is the IBA recipe:

- 1 ounce Calvados
- 1 ounce gin
- 1 ounce apricot brandy

Shake all ingredients with ice and strain contents into a cocktail glass.

DELLA MELA

This long drink, created by Jackson Cannon at the Hawthorne and Eastern Standard in Boston, features the brown, bitter-orange-flavored Italian soda called chinotto, which turns out to be a perfect companion for Calvados. It allows for a wonderful apple flavor to shine through.

- Ice
- 1 1/2 ounces Calvados
- 3 to 4 ounces chinotto soda, preferably San Pellegrino brand
- 1 round, thin orange slice, for garnish

Fill a highball glass with ice. Add the Calvados and the chinotto soda and stir gently to combine. Garnish with the orange slice.

CALVADOS HIGHBALL

Calvados on ice has never been a tradition in Normandy but I have noticed consumers enjoying young Calvados with ice cubes in a number of countries, including Spain, the United States, and Japan. Served on ice in long drinks, Calvados contributes its apple aromas generously to ginger beer, ginger ale, and tonic water — or simply club soda, which creates a harmonious match with the magic of bubbles. One could say that the pre-war tradition of "Fine à l'eau" is coming back as a highball drink.

Jack Rose cocktail

1 ½ ounces Calvados
3 ounces club soda or seltzer
Apple peel spiral, for garnish

Fill a tall, narrow-mouthed glass with ice. Pour in the Calvados, then top with club soda or seltzer and garnish with the apple peel.

NORMANDY HIGHBALL

Tomoaki Wasai, Calvados ambassador and the owner of Bar Stag at Kitakyushu-shi, Fukuoka, proposes the following variation on the Calvados highball:

1 ½ ounces Calvados
3 drops orange bitters
3 ounces club soda or seltzer
Orange peel, for garnish

In a tall, narrow-mouthed glass, combine one ounce of Calvados with the orange bitters. Stir to combine, then top with soda water followed by ice. Top the drink with the remaining Calvados, then garnish with the orange peel.

THE NORMAN MULE

Tasty and refreshing!

1.5 ounces of Calvados
3 ounces ginger beer
One dash of Angostura bitters
Twist of lemon, for garnish

Fill a tall glass with ice. Pour in the Calvados and top with ginger beer. Add the Angostura and stir gently. Garnish with a twist of lemon.

WIDOW'S KISS

This cocktail, first created in the late 19th century by George Kappeler, involves two French liquors with romantic and mysterious company stories. Dating back to 1510, Benedictine is believed to be the world's oldest liqueur. Made from brandy and a secret infusion of herbs, the recipe is closely guarded at the Benedictine abbey in Fecamp, Normandy. Chartreuse is made in the Alpine town of Voiron at a monastery called La Grande Chartreuse. There is little chance its secret recipe will ever be revealed. The only two Carthusian monks who know it have taken a vow of silence.

Ice
1 1/2 ounces Calvados
3/4 ounce Benedictine liqueur
3/4 ounce yellow Chartreuse liqueur
1 dash Angostura bitters
1 strawberry, for garnish

Fill a cocktail shaker two-thirds full with ice and add the Calvados, liqueurs, and bitters. Shake vigorously, then strain into a chilled martini glass. Drop in the strawberry and serve.

PHILADELPHIA SCOTCHMAN

Calvados with Port, orange juice, and ginger beer? Odd, but delicious. The early 20th century recipe for this cocktail called for applejack and ginger ale, but spicier ginger beer and Calvados work much better. Any good ruby or younger light tawny Port works.

The reason behind the drink's obscure and puzzling name is mostly lost to history. It might be in honor of Hughie Hutchinson, a successful boxer who had that nickname (and died of pneumonia at age 22).

- Ice cubes
- 3/4 ounce Calvados
- 3/4 ounce port
- 3/4 ounce freshly squeezed orange juice
- 1 ounce chilled ginger beer

Fill a rocks or old-fashioned glass with ice. Add the apple brandy, Port, and orange juice. Stir, then top with the chilled ginger beer.

CALVADOS SOUR

This drink first appeared in William Schmidt's 1892 cocktail book The Flowing Bowl.

Few drinks are simpler and more appealing than a real sour, meaning one that uses freshly squeezed lemon juice and simple syrup instead of artificial sour mix. You can make a sour with just about any spirit, but it's perfect with Calvados. Here is a variation proposed by Jason Wilson.

- Ice
- 1 ounce freshly squeezed lemon juice
- ½ ounce simple syrup
- 1½ ounces Calvados
- Preserved or maraschino cherry, for garnish

Fill a cocktail shaker halfway with ice. Add the lemon juice, simple syrup and brandy. Shake well, then strain into a rock or old fashioned glass. Garnish with the cherry.

Calvados Sour

APPLE SUNRISE

Here's a Calvados-fueled twist on the classic Tequila Sunrise, the original of which always called for creme de cassis instead of the grenadine that's mostly used now. Look for true creme de cassis from Dijon, France.

- Ice cubes
- ¼ ounce freshly squeezed lemon juice
- ¼ ounce creme de cassis (see headnote)
- 1½ ounces Calvados
- 2 ounces freshly squeezed orange juice

Fill a highball or Collins glass with ice. Pour the lemon juice into the glass, then the creme de cassis, then the brandy and finally the orange juice. Stir gently.

CALVADOS TODDY

Apple toddies were all the rage in pre-Prohibition America, and they're even better with Calvados. They're delicious, and worth the effort it takes to bake the apples (peeled and cored, in a 325-degree oven for about 30 minutes until softened). The drinks can be assembled right in the mugs (half an apple for each portion), but the toddy is nicer when you strain out the apple bits.

To make 4 servings:

- 15 ounces (2 cups minus 2 tablespoons) hot water, just boiled, plus more to warm the mugs
- 4 teaspoons sugar
- 2 peeled and cored baked apples (see headnote)

    6 ounces Calvados
    Freshly grated nutmeg, for garnish (optional)

Warm four mugs with a little of the just-boiled water; swirl and discard. Combine the sugar with a splash (about one ounce) of the just-boiled water in a medium bowl, stirring to dissolve. Add the baked apples and muddle them thoroughly. Add the Calvados and mix well, then stir in 12 ounces of the water.

Use a fine-mesh strainer to immediately strain equal portions of the liquid into the four mugs, discarding the solids. Top each portion with 1/2 ounce of hot water, and stir. Sprinkle with nutmeg, if desired. Serve immediately.

STAR COCKTAIL

Harry's ABC of Mixing Cocktails, *published in New York in 1911, calls for one teaspoon each of grapefruit Juice, dry vermouth, sweet vermouth, and then an unspecified amount of base spirit, split in equal parts between gin and Calvados. Difford's guide adapts this historical recipe as follows:*

    1 ½ ounces Calvados
    1 ½ ounces sweet vermouth
    1 dash Angostura bitters
    Olive, for garnish

Stir all ingredients with ice and strain into a chilled cocktail glass. Garnish with an olive.

THE FRENCH 75

Named after the 75-millimeter light field French gun, the original recipe was created in 1915 at the New York Bar in Paris. MacElhone's recipe consisted of Calvados, gin, grenadine and Absinthe:

    ⅔ ounce Calvados
    ⅓ ounce gin
    1 teaspoon grenadine
    Two dashes absinthe.

Combine all ingredients in a shaker filled with ice. Shake, then strain into a chilled cocktail glass.

If you order a "French 75" today, however, there is a good chance that you will get a cocktail of gin, lemon juice and simple syrup shaken with ice and topped with sparkling wine!

HONEYMOON COCKTAIL

The Honeymoon Cocktail is an apple brandy sour which appeared in 1916 in Hugo Ensslin's book, Recipes for Mixed Drinks, *where it was offered in Applejack and Calvados versions. It attained widespread popularity when the Brown Derby restaurant in Los Angeles featured it on the menu.*

    2 ounces Calvados
    ½ ounce Benedictine
    ½ ounce orange Curaçao
    ½ ounce freshly squeezed lemon juice
    Lemon peel, for garnish

Combine Calvados, Benedictine, orange Curaçao, and lemon juice in a cocktail shaker filled with ice. Shake and strain into a chilled cocktail glass. Garnish with lemon peel.

CORPSE REVIVER NO.1
A creation of Frank Meir, the bar manager at the Ritz Bar in Paris, the Corpse Reviver No. 1 was immortalized in The Savoy Cocktail Book, *which stated it should "be taken before 11am, or whenever steam and energy are needed."*

- ¾ ounce Calvados
- 1½ ounce Cognac
- ¾ ounce sweet vermouth

Combine all ingredients in a shaker filled with ice. Shake, then strain into a chilled cocktail glass.

BLOCK AND FALL
The original recipe for the Block and Fall was created by T. Van Dycke at Ciro's Club in Deauville in 1924. The following recipe is from Harry's ABC of Mixing Cocktails.

- ¾ ounce Calvados
- ¾ ounce Cognac
- ¾ ounce Cointreau
- ½ ounce anisette

Combine all ingredients in a shaker filled with ice. Shake, then strain into a chilled cocktail glass.

THE PINK LADY OR THE SECRET COCKTAIL
Jim Meehan, founder of PDT, is a big fan of serving Calvados in fall and winter cocktails. He says that Drouin Calvados makes for a great swap in cocktail recipes such as the Pink Lady, which typically calls for applejack. He's also quick to point out that this is a one-way street: there's no substitute for a great French brandy. He created this recipe in 2013.

- 1 ounce Junipero Gin
- 1 ounce Drouin Selection Calvados
- ¾ ounce lemon juice
- ¾ ounce grenadine
- 1 egg white

Combine all ingredients in a shaker without ice. Dry shake to froth the egg white, then add a scoop of ice and shake again to chill. Strain into a chilled coupe.

THE CALVADOS COCKTAIL
From the Savoy Cocktail Book.

- 1½ ounces Calvados
- 1½ ounces orange juice
- ¾ ounce Cointreau
- ¾ ounce orange bitters
- Sugar, for garnish.

Lightly moisten the rim of a cocktail glass with orange juice, then dip into sugar to create a sugar rim.

Combine all other ingredients in a shaker filled with ice. Shake, then strain into garnished glass.

THE GOLDEN DAWN
This pre-dinner cocktail was created by Thomas Buttery, then head barman of London's Berkeley Hotel. It was judged the "World's Finest Cocktail" at the United Kingdom Bartenders' Guild (UKBG) International Cocktail Competition in London in 1930.

- ¾ ounce Calvados,
- ¾ ounce dry gin,
- ¾ ounce apricot brandy
- ¾ ounce freshly squeezed orange juice
- 1 dash pomegranate grenadine
- Cherry, for garnish

Combine all ingredients except the pomegranate grenadine in a shaker filled with ice. Shake, then strain into a cocktail glass. Add a dash of pomegranate grenadine after the cocktail is poured, then drop a stemless cherry into the drink as garnish. Do not stir.

DIKI-DIKI COCKTAIL
This drink was invented by Robert Vermière, who first published it in his 1922 book Cocktails: How To Mix Them. *It later appeared in* The Savoy Cocktail Book.

- 1 ½ ounces Calvados
- ½ ounce Swedish Punsch
- ¾ ounce freshly squeezed grapefruit juice
- Sugar, for garnish

Lightly moisten the rim of a chilled cocktail glass with grapefruit juice, then dip into sugar to create a sugar rim.
Shake all other ingredients with ice and strain into garnished cocktail glass.

▶ Classic Cocktails Revisited

Bartenders have developed many variations on classic cocktails by replacing Calvados with other spirits, or replacing the original spirit in a recipe with Calvados. Here are some popular examples of the latter.

Apple Mojito

JACK COLLINS
Collins are sours with the addition of soda water, making them longer and more refreshing. The basic Collins ingredients are lemon juice, powdered sugar, sparkling water, and a spirit base. While the Tom Collins calls for gin, a Jack Collins replaces the gin with Calvados.

- 1 ½ ounces Calvados
- ¾ ounce freshly squeezed lemon juice
- One tablespoon powdered sugar
- Soda water
- Lemon wheel, for garnish

Combine Calvados, lemon juice, and sugar in a tall Collins glass. Stir to combine, then add ice cubes and top with soda water. Garnish with lemon wheel.

APPLE MOJITO
This popular Cuban cocktail, which dates back to the Prohibition period, is simply a rum Collins garnished with sprigs of mint. Replace the rum with Calvados, however, to obtain an apple mojito. Young Calvados or La Blanche deliver a subtle apple flavor without too much oak, while the combination of mint, lime, and sparkling water is a recipe for pure refreshment. Here is

a variation created by Marc Jean, President of ABF Normandy, for Calvados Domaine Dupont.

- 10 fresh mint leaves, plus extra for garnish
- 1 lime, quartered
- ⅓ ounce simple syrup
- ½ tsp powdered sugar
- 1 ½ ounce Calvados
- 2 ½ ounce ginger ale

Combine mint leaves, lime quarters, simple syrup, and powdered sugar in a tumbler and muddle well. Fill the tumbler with ice cubes, add Calvados, and top with the ginger ale. Stir gently and garnish with fresh mint.

APPLE MANHATTAN

The original Manhattan calls for rye whiskey, but here it is replaced by Calvados. Old Calvados and dry vermouth will give excellent results for this cocktail, as will a Perfect variation, which replaces the sweet vermouth with a split base of ½ ounce sweet vermouth and ½ ounce dry vermouth.

- 2 ounces Calvados
- 1 ounce sweet vermouth
- 2 dashes Angostura bitters
- Maraschino cherry, for garnish

Stir Calvados, vermouth, and bitters with ice until well chilled, about 30 seconds. Strain into a chilled cocktail glass and garnish with the cherry.

APPLE SIDECAR

The sidecar was popularized by Harry's Bar in Paris. The following recipe is a simple variation on the classic, which was originally made with Cognac.

- 1 ½ ounces Calvados
- 1 ounce French cider
- 1 ounce orange liqueur
- 1 ounce freshly squeezed lemon or lime juice
- Apple slice, for garnish

Combine all ingredients except garnish in an ice-filled shaker. Shake and strain into a chilled martini glass. Garnish with the apple slice.

APPLE NEGRONI

One of the most popular Italian cocktails, the Negroni was allegedly created by Count Camillo Negroni in 1919 at the Caffè Casoni in Florence, Italy, when he ordered an Americano made with gin instead of soda water. La Blanche, a young calvados, or even an apple gin also give remarkable results.

- 1 ounce Calvados
- 1 ounce Italian vermouth rosso (red, semi-sweet)
- 1 ounce Campari
- 1 slice of orange, for garnish

Pour all the ingredients except the garnish directly into an old fashioned glass filled with ice. Stir to chill, and garnish with the orange.

▶ Cocktails From the Dark Era

It wasn't all Long Island Iced Teas and Cosmopolitans. Here are some Calvados recipes created during the late 20th century.

SERENDIPITY

Peter Colin Field, a true Calvados aficionado, put his talent at work at the Hemingway bar at the Ritz Paris. The Serendipity, which he created in 1994, is a Hemingway Bar Signature and Colin Field's very favorite cocktail. "This is an important cocktail as it represents France in your glass," he says. 30 years later, this modern cocktail has become a new classic.

> ¾ ounce Christian Drouin VSOP Calvados or Calvados Pays d'Auge Original.
> ½ teaspoon of sugar
> 2 fresh mint stalks
> 1 ounce clear apple juice from Normandy
> 2 ounces Champagne

Combine Calvados, sugar, mint, apple juice, and ice in a tumbler. Stir to combine and top with Champagne.

NORMANDY

This simple cocktail was also created by Peter Colin Field in 1994. It marks the 50th anniversary of Paris' liberation.

> 1 ½ ounce Calvados Pays d'Auge Original
> 1 ounce Pommeau Christian Drouin

Stir Calvados and Pommeau with ice, then strain into a chilled old fashioned glass filled with ice.

Serendipity

MERIDIEN 30

This dessert drink was created by Lucien Dulac at the bar of the Hotel Meridien in Paris to commemorate its 30th anniversary.

> 1 ⅓ ounce Calvados cream
> ⅔ ounce amaretto
> ⅔ ounce coffee cream liqueur
> ⅓ ounce fresh cream
> One dash orange essence
> Cocoa powder, for ganish

Combine Calvados, Amaretto, and coffee cream in a shaker filled with ice. Stir to chill, then strain into a cocktail glass. Top with the cream, orange essence, and a dusting of cocoa powder.

▶ **Craft Cocktails**

I read somewhere that "if palace bars rather tend to be classic-minded with a zest of craziness, proportions are inverted at trendy spots." Trendsetting mixologists, most of the time tending to base their drinks on the classics, often combine previously unpaired ingredients, attempt new infusions, incorporate tea and coffee, and use the best of what fruits and vegetables are in season.

Many of these cocktails use infusions and other compounds prepared by the mixologist. Although they are not necessarily meant to be reproduced, I present some emblematic modern Calvados-based recipes to give inspiration to creative bartenders.

SPINEY APPLE

I met Sean Ludford for the first time years ago when he was selecting spirits at Sam's in Chicago. He is the creator of BeverageExperts.com and a quarterly magazine, and is a true Calvados connoisseur. Here is a relatively simple recipe he proposed in BevX in 2009:

1 ounce añejo Tequila
1 ounce Calvados
2 ounces high-quality ginger beer

Combine Calvados and Tequila in a rocks glass with a healthy handful of ice. Stir, then top with the ginger beer, stirring gently to combine.

APPLE BLOSSOM

In The Dead Rabbit Grocery and Grog Drinks Manual, *I found some interesting recipes such as this one, which was inspired by a recipe from William Schmidt's* The Flowing Bowl, *published in 1892, and the following recipe for the Parisian, which was inspired by J.A. Grohusko's 1908 book,* Jack's Manual of Recipes for Fancy Mixed Drinks and How To Serve Them.

2 ounces strawberry-infused Calvados
½ oz strawberry cordial
1 oz fresh lemon juice
¾ oz Combier pink grapefruit
3 dashes Bittermens Hopped grapefruit bitters

Combine all ingredients in a chaker filled with ice. Shake, then strain into a chilled glass.

PARISIAN

1 ½ ounce Byrrh Grand Quinquina
1 ½ ounce Château du Breuil VSOP Calvados
½ ounce Combier Crème de cassis
3 dashes Bittermens Burlesque Bitters
3 ounces Christian Drouin Cidre Bouché
Lemon peel, for garnish

Add all ingredients except the Cidre Bouché and lemon peel to a mixing glass filled with ice. Stir until chilled. Add the Cidre Bouché, and strain the mixture into an ice-filled wine glass. Twist the lemon peel over the glass to express the oils, then discard the peel.

Three cocktails from New York, offered for inspiration:

- Home Run
The Dead Rabbit, New York,
Scotch, Calvados, Amaro, Brown Rice Tea, Cinnamon, Pineapple, lime.

- The Milk of Sorrow
Nomo Soho, New York
Calvados, Amontillado Sherry, Way & Nephew Rum OVP Pine Nuts Orgeat, Lime, Angostura Bitters.

- The Pfaffle
The Vault at Pfaff's, New York

Drouin Selection Calvados, house infused cinnamon Vodka, muddled red delicious apple, fresh nutmeg.

LE POM'POM

In 2014, the IDAC (Interprofession des Appellations Cidricoles)asked three top Parisian mixologists, Sullivan Doh, Michael Mas, and Thomas Girard to create a new Calvados based cocktail with potential to be world class. The result was le Pom'Pom

6 or 7 pink peppercorns

Pom Pom

3 fresh basil leaves
2/3 ounce sugar syrup
2/3 ounce fresh lemon juice
1 ¼ ounce Calvados
1 ounce sparkling water
Ice cubes

Muddle the pink peppercorns in a shaker. Add basil leaves, torn into pieces. Add the sugar syrup, lemon juice and Calvados. Fill the shaker with ice and shake, then strain into a cocktail glass filled with ice. Top with sparkling water.

AN APPLE A DAY

This cocktail, from Calvados Christian Drouin's Calvados Cocktails Inspiration, *was created by Emily Reynolds at Little Red Door in Paris. "The sherry is fairly dry, with an herbaceous side that goes well with the nose of Calvados and fenouillette, a liquor from the south. The malic acid increases the acidity of the cocktail, and the tonic water accentuates its freshness and the herbaceous side," says Reynolds,*

1 ounce Calvados Christian Drouin Selection
⅔ ounce Manzanilla sherry
½ ounce Fenouillette
Tonic water, for topping
Seasonal edible flowers, for garnish (optional)

Combine Calvados, sherry, and fenouillette in a highball glass. Stir to combine, top with ice, and stir again to chill. Top with tonic water. Garnish with optional flowers.

Above — An Apple a Day
Below — Kashaval

LE 14130

This cocktail was created by Margot Le Carpentier at Combat in Paris and originally published in Calvados Cocktails Inspiration. *"This cocktail pays tribute to the Drouin distillery, as the name is Coudray-Rabut postal code," she explains. "I drew inspiration from a conventional daiquiri, using gum arabic syrup to provide texture thickness. I strongly associate radish with apple, so I make a radish shrub with a dash of vinegar that I mix with the gum. The nori garnish accentuates the radish."*

1 ⅓ ounce Calvados Christian Drouin Selection
½ ounce gum arabic syrup
1 ounce freshly squeezed lime juice
1 teaspoon white radish shrub
Sesame seeds and nori sheet, for garnish

Combine all ingredients except for sesame seeds and nori in a shaker filled with ice. Shake vigorously, then strain into a chilled coupe. Garnish with sesame seeds and nori.

KASHAVAL

Originally published in Calvados Cocktails Inspiration, *the Kashaval was created by Clément Emery at Le Bar Botaniste in Paris. He says that the combination of Calvados and roasted buckwheat provides richness, while the Pommeau and cider add complexity and smoothness and the walnut wine evokes rancio.*

1 ⅔ ounce Calvados Christian Drouin Selection infused with buckwheat
⅔ ounce cider vinegar
⅔ ounce Vieux Pommeau
½ ounce walnut wine

⅔ ounce egg white
Extra brut cider, for topping
Apple blossom, for garnish (optional)

Combine Calvados, cider vinegar, pommeau, walnut wine, and egg white in a shaker without ice. Shake vigorously to froth the egg white, then add ice and shake again to chill. Strain into a chilled glass, then top with cider. Garnish with optional apple blossom.

▶ La Blanche Cocktails

La Blanche excels in cocktails — as evidenced by its outstanding performance in cocktail competitions. In London, at the respected Drinks International Bartender Challenge (DIBC) in 2007, Anne Dubois was awarded the trophy in the "White Spirits —Long Drink" category for her Sticking Around, and a Gold Medal in the "White Spirits — Aperitif" category for her Blanche Dubois, two cocktails that used La Blanche as a base.

In Japan, at the 15th Nippon Bartenders Association Junior Cocktail competition in 2010, Mr. Isoda from Osaka won the Grand Prix with La Blanche as a base in his original cocktail, which called for one ounce of La Blanche, 1/3 ounce Maraschino liqueur, 1/3 ounce green banana syrup, and 1/3 ounce fresh lime juice — with the directions kept secret!

Many recipes have been created all over the world using La Blanche as the base spirit. Here are a few to give inspiration:

POM-SENSE
This recipe was created to highlight La Blanche, and was sent to me by American bartender Ryan McGinnis.

1 ½ ounce La Blanche,
3 ounces Sence Rose Nectar (juice made from rose petals)
½ ounce fresh squeezed lemon juice (about half a lemon)
⅓ ounce sugar syrup
Sugar, for garnish

Rim a cocktail glass with sugar.
Combine all other ingredients in a shaker with ice. Shake, then strain into the sugar-rimmed cocktail glass.

CAIPI CALVA JAM
This recipe was contributed by Diego Ferrari in Milan.

30 grams apple jelly
1 lime
2 ⅓ ounce La Blanche

Chop the lime into pieces and muddle in a tumbler with the jelly. Add the La Blanche, stir, and top with crushed ice.

THE GOLDEN LION
The Golden Lion was created by Marc Bonneton in one of the best-known French speakeasy bars, l'Antiquaire in Lyon.

1 ¾ ounce La Blanche
⅔ ounce lemon juice
⅓ ounce sugar syrup
1 dash of orange bitters

1/6 ounce Absinthe
Orange peel, for garnish

Combine all ingredients except garnish in a shaker filled with ice. Shake, then strain into a chilled cocktail glass. Garnish with orange peel.

LA MELA

This cocktail was created by Diane Vanderbrouke at Mary Celeste in Paris for Calvados Cocktails Inspiration. "I opted for a La Blanche base with a twist of Jack Rose and a Mary Celeste touch," she says.

1 2/3 ounce La Blanche
2/3 ounce egg white
3/4 ounce lemon
2 1/2 ounces Nardini Acqua di Cedro
1/2 ounce Nardini Rabarbaro
2 dashes Peychaud's bitters, for garnish

Combine all ingredients except bitters in a shaker without ice. Shake vigorously to froth the egg white, then add ice and shake again to chill. Double-strain into a large chilled coupe, and garnish with two dashes of bitters.

FORD HARRISON

The Ford Harrison was created by Margot Le Carpentier at Combat in Paris for Calvados Cocktails Inspiration. She describes it as "a cocktail that can be drunk as an aperitif, or for dessert if you like dry, slightly saline cocktails."

1 ounce La Blanche,
1/2 ounce Nikka Coffey Malt infused with toasted bread
1/2 ounce Dolin dry vermouth
1/2 ounce Barolo chinato
1/3 ounce Benedictine
1 tsp green olive brine

Combine all ingredients in a shaker filled with ice. Stir to chill, then strain into a chilled coupe.

▶ Pommeau de Normandie cocktails

In mixology, Pommeau de Normandie can be used as an alternative to some vermouths. It also mixes very well with Champagne and gin.

POMMEAU ROYAL

This cocktail was created by Jean-Paul Thomine at Casino de Deauville, and was published in 1992 in Pommeau de Normandie, *from Charles Corlet Editions.*

1 1/3 ounce Pommeau
1 ounce Cointreau
1/3 ounce lemon juice
Champagne, to top

Combine Pommeau, Cointreau, and lemon juice in a shaker filled with ice. Shake, then strain into a flute and top with Champagne.

POMMEAU ANNABELLE

This cocktail was created by Hilmar Gathoff at the restaurant Habel am Reichstag in Berlin for my visit. It has since become popular in Germany.

- 1½ ounce Pommeau de Normandie
- 3 ounces Prosecco or Sekt
- Brown sugar, for garnish
- Baby apple, for garnish

Rim a champagne flute with brown sugar. Pour the Pommeau into the flute and add the apple, ideally speared with a decorative cocktail stick. Top with Prosecco or Sekt.

LE VRAI NORMAND

This cocktail was created by Jean-Paul Thomine, the former president of the Norman Bartenders Association.

- 1 ounce Calvados
- ⅔ ounce Pommeau
- 2 ounces apple juice
- ⅓ ounce grenadine

Combine all ingredients in a shaker filled with ice. Stir to chill, then strain into a tumbler filled with fresh ice.

Calvados Producers

WHILE CALVADOS WAS PRODUCED for centuries by thousands of farmers and marketed to a large number by negociants and cooperatives, it is now made by many fewer producers. In the 1970s and 1980s, the spirits giants showed interest in the category. Then, they decided to withdraw in favor of categories that were easier to produce. In the seventies, main negociants such as Boulard or Magloire switched to distillation, buying apples or cider rather than spirits as they used to do.

In 2018, there were still more than 6,000 fruit growers and 453 producer-growers, distillers and merchants. Fifteen companies make up more than 93% of Calvados' total sales, while ten companies are responsible for 97% of export sales. In the Pays d'Auge Appellation, there are 59 producers and 3,252 hectares of orchards. In the Domfrontais Appellation, there are 57 producers and 752 hectares of orchards, and in the Calvados Appellation there are 337 producers and 7,329 hectares of orchards. One can say that today there is no bad Calvados, only good Calvados, better ones, and great ones.

The main brands of Calvados, as well as most craft producers, can be found in the United States. Here is a brief list of the houses exporting to the United States as per the list released by IDAC, to which I added a few names which were not on the list but whose bottles I saw in the United States. This list may not be complete.

Some brands belong to a group, such as Busnel, which is owned by La Martiniquaise, or Boulard, Magloire, and Lecompte, three brands owned by Spirit France. Domaine du Coquerel, which was owned by an international group for years, has turned into a family business again and belongs to the Martin family. The largest sales volumes are marketed by these brands. With significant volumes to sell, their products are enjoyed by the mainstream.

Then come family-owned estates — some of which have existed for several generations — cooperatives, and independent bottlers, who select Calvados barrels from distilleries and farmers. Spirits made by smaller producers usually reflect the personality and taste of the owner and target premium markets. Most of them are faithful to ancestral traditions, while some are innovative in their quest for excellence.

Brands Belonging to Groups

La Martiniquaise: Calvados Busnel and Anée

In 1970, Pernod Ricard bought Les Distilleries Réunies, an industrial distillery built in 1910 in Cormeilles. They later bought Calvados Busnel, a family company located in Pont-L'Evêque whose origins can be traced back to 1820, and acquired another family company, Anée, founded in 1919 by George Anée and located in Vimoutiers. Busnel and Anée were then gathered in Cormeilles and the distillery name became Busnel. In 2003 Pernod Ricard sold the company to La Martiniquaise, the largest Calvados producer and current owner. Busnel also markets Calvados under other brand names, such as Papidoux.

Spirit France: Boulard, Père Magloire, Lecompte

In 2007, a Russian businessman, Timur Goryayev, acquired these three brands from the Pellerin and Boulard families. The transaction went through an investment fund, Spirit Capital, based in Switzerland (the operation was completed in 2011). They constitute the second-largest Calvados producer in volume. Since the cidery in Pont L'Evêque was sold, the group has not produced any cider.

In the 1970s, Boulard and Magloire switched from their traditional merchant business to distillation. Calvados marketed under Boulard, Père Magloire, and Lecompte brands is now distilled in Coquainvilliers. Since 2017, they have been aging, bottling, and shipping the three brands in the same huge and modern warehouse in Reux near Pont-L'Evêque. In 2018, Spirit France inaugurated the "Calvados Experience," a virtual high-tech Calvados museum in Pont-L'Evêque.

Calvados Boulard

The origins of Calvados Boulard company go back to 1825 when Messrs. Decaux and Lacaille started a wine spirit warehouse in Yvetôt. In 1875, Pierre Auguste Boulard bought the company and started selling cider spirit. The company remained a family company until 1987. With the exception of one small production activity before WWII, it also remained an independent bottler. In 1970, Boulard acquired La Distillerie du Moulin de la Foulonnerie in Coquainvilliers. The head office, warehouse, and bottling facilities remained in Yvetot. From 1977 to 1980, a low stem orchard of 65 hectares was planted in Ouilly du Houley.

In 1987, due to inheritance problems, the family had to sell the company to Saint Raphaël, part of the Martini & Rossi group. Martini & Rossi acquired La Benedictine in Fecamp and gathered Boulard and La Benedictine facilities from Yvetôt to Tourville les Ifs. This was the end of 163 years in Yvetôt. Martini & Rossi made substantial investments in Boulard, buying a cidery in Pont-L'Evêque in 1991 and building a new distillery in Coquainvilliers. Then Bacardi took over Martini & Rossi and decided not to keep Calvados Boulard. In 1996, Yves Pellerin, owner of Calvados Lecompte in Notre Dame de Courson, decided to purchase the company. Together with Lecompte and Père Magloire, Boulard was sold to Spirit Capital in 2008.

Boulard is the largest exporter of Calvados Pays d'Auge. The company also sells Calvados under other brands such as Dauphin, Dumanoir, Norois, and Jehan Foucart.

Calvados Père Magloire

Père Magloire was one of the first known Calvados brands. Its history, which can be traced back to 1821, is complicated. In 1960, Debrise Dulac acquired the brand from the Bizouard family, as well as a piece of land in Pont-L'Evêque to build a warehouse. From 1963 to 2017, Calvados Père Magloire was aged and bottled in Pont-L'Evêque. Calvados was supplied thanks to a partnership with Anée in Vimoutiers and Sallin in Sainte-Foy-de Montgommery. In 1974, the Distillery de la Vie was inaugurated next to the cidery and distillery of Sainte-Foy-de-Montgommery

In 1968, Debrise-Dulac, Père Magloire 's owner, was taken over by Champagne Veuve Clicquot Ponsardin which, in turn, was bought by Louis Vuitton Moët Hennessy (LVMH) in 1988. In 1998, Yves Pellerin, owner of Calvados Lecompte, and his son Benoit bought Père Magloire from LVMH through Pays d'Auge Finance, building another large Calvados group.

The distillery in Sainte-Foix de Montgomery has been closed. Calvados is now distilled in Coquinvilliers and aged in Reux warehouse.

Calvados Lecompte

Lecompte tends to be the group's most traditional brand, thus reflecting its origins. The history of Lecompte goes back to 1923, when Alexandre Lecompte started selling Calvados under the family name. The facilities were located in Lisieux. In 1979, after the death of Pierre, Alexandre Lecompte's son Yves Pellerin bought the firm and soon acquired from Mr. Fontaine his distillery and farm with its stock of old Calvados in Notre-Dame-de-Courson, where he then moved production.

In 2007, the Pellerin family sold the whole group to Spirit France. In 2018, Spirit France decided to close the distillery in Notre Dame de Courson and move the stock to Coquainvilliers warehouse.

▶ Medium-Sized, Family-Owned Producers

Domaine du Coquerel

Founded by the Gilbert family in 1937, Domaine du Coquerel soon became one of the leading Calvados houses by volume. In 1971, the German brandy company Asbach bought Gilbert and turned it into one of the major brands in Germany. Initially sold as Calvados Gilbert, the Calvados was renamed Coquerel. After Asbach's sale to Guinness

Manoir du Coquerel

in 1995, Jean-Francois Martin bought the Calvados firm back from Guinness. Today, Domaine du Coquerel is located in Milly, not far from Mont Saint Michel, and is run by Pierre Martin Neuhaus, Jean-Francois Martin's son.

Calvados is marketed under the Coquerel, Marquis de la Pomme, and Morice brand names. In addition to Calvados they also produce Normindia Gin. The company also sells products under other brand names, such as Berneroy.

Avallen Spirits is a new Calvados brand created in 2019 by two ex-Diagio brand ambassadors, Stephanie Jordan and Tim Etherington-Judge, and produced at the Coquerel distillery. Avallen was inspired by the fact that Calvados is the most planet-positive spirit. Designed for mixing, Avallen is a Calvados for bartenders to infuse into their libations.

Château du Breuil

In 1954, Philippe Bizouard bought the castle of Le Breuil-en-Auge from Count Pierre Grouard de Tocqueville and founded the Bizouard du Breuil company (BDB). The idea was to name the Calvados after the castle. He created an elegant and original bottle that made the brand easy to identify on a trolley or a shelf. In 1987, wishing to retire, he sold the company to the Swiss company Diwisa, which made important investments in orchards and facilities. Bizouard du Breuil was then renamed Château du Breuil SA. The Affentranger family, who founded Diwisa in 1918, sold the company in 2014 but kept Château du Breuel as an independent family-owned company. In the middle of a 28-hectare estate, the castle, built in the 16th and 17th centuries, is one of Normandy's architectural treasures. In 2020, the company was sold to Frederic Dussart and Roberto Montesano, and became La Spiriterie.

The estate owns 42 hectares of orchards which provide approximately 40% of its requirements. The remaining fruits are bought from 120 suppliers. They exclusively produce Calvados Pays d'Auge.

Calvados Christian Drouin

In 1960, Christian Drouin senior bought a farm located in Gonneville-sur-Honfleur in Pays d'Auge called Les Fiefs Sainte Anne as a country house. The farm was planted with cider apple trees, so Christian Drouin decided to produce his own Calvados. With the help of Pierre Pivet, a licensed distiller well known in Pays d'Auge, he spent twenty years distilling his cider production. The resulting Calvados was set aside to age in former sherry, Port and Calvados casks stored in the old half-timbered outbuildings of the farm. He also acquired batches of very old Calvados when the estates of some reputed producers were sold.

In 1969, Christian Drouin Junior went into partnership with his father, but it was only in 1979 that stocks were considered sufficient to allow marketing to begin. At the beginning, Calvados was offered under the brand "Coeur de Lion", after King Richard the Lion Heart. In the early 2000s, it was decided to sell it under the founder's name.

In 1991-92, to meet the need for more space, Christian Drouin Junior transferred most of the production to a 17th century estate in Coudray-Rabut near Pont-l'Evêque that he carefully restored. In 1990-92, to secure a source of supply of Domfrontais Calvados, he made a joint venture with Les Chais du Verger Normand in Domfront.

In 2004, the third generation joined the company: Guillaume Drouin, trained as agricultural engineer and winemaker. In 2013 Guillaume was appointed Chief Executive Officer. In 2017, the company acquired Calvados Lelouvier after the death of Christian Lelouvier, a independent bottler specialized in high-end AOC Calvados.

Organic apples are supplied by the high stem orchards at the farm in Gonneville sur Honfleur and supplemented by neighboring farms. Cider is produced on the farm in Gonneville sur Honfleur using a pneumatic press, and distilled in a 25hl new pot still in Coudray-Rabut. Calvados is aged in small oak casks of various origins. In addition to calvados, Drouin produces an apple gin and an aperitif made from Calvados called ABC.

Drouin also markets Calvados under the Marquis de Saint Loup and Chevalier des Touches brands.

Domaine Familial Louis Dupont

In 1916, Jules Dupont bought the estate he was leasing where he produced Calvados. In 1934, his son Louis succeeded his father. In 1974 after Louis' death, his widow Colette managed the Domaine. In 1980, after living abroad, Etienne Dupont, the fourth generation, returned to the property.

The estate totals 27 hectares. Etienne transformed the traditional activity by planting low stem orchards with more spacing than many, maturing the fruit in wooden boxes (pallox), and using a large percentage of new oak casks to age the Calvados. Then, the fifth generation, Jérôme, joined Etienne. Jérôme Dupont, an innovator like his father, sadly passed away too soon in 2018. Etienne and Jerome contributed to make Calvados better-known worldwide. Domaine Familial Louis Dupont is also well-known for its cider

Calvados Roger Groult

In the eighteenth century, the family Groult settled in Le Clos de la Hurvanière, located in St Cyr du Ronceray near Orbec in Pays d'Auge. Cow breeding, milk, and, of course, cider production were the main activities on the estate.

Five generations ago, Pierre Groult (1830-1918) started to distill his cider and age it in oak barrels, and Calvados Groult was born. After him, each generation developed Calvados production until it became the only activity on the estate. The estate totals 24 hectares of orchards (15 hectares of traditional high-stems and 9 hectares of "half-stem" apple trees. A few selected local farmers also supply their apple harvests to complement the estate production. Today the traditions are perpetuated by Estelle Groult, who maintains very traditional methods of production: apples ciders are distilled after one year of slow and natural fermentation, double-distillation takes place over wood fire in three small pot-stills, and spirit is aged in very old oak barrels.

Calvados

Since 1865, the Huet family has produced cider and Calvados at the La Brière des Fontaines, a manor in Cambremer. The fruits (more than 25 apples varieties as well as pears) come from 20 hectares of low-stem orchards and 10 hectares of traditional orchards. They also buy apples from nearby farmers. They double distill over wood fire and age their Calvados in barrels of various sizes and origins. Woodchips produced on the estate serve as ecological fuel. They also produce AOC Calvados using a column still heated with woodchips. The fifth generation of producers, Cyril Marchand-Huet and François Xavier Huet, joined Philippe Huet after Pierre Huet's death in 2004.

▶ Pays d'Auge Farmer Producers

Manoir d'Apreval

Victor Revillon acquired the Manoir d'Apreval Domaine at the beginning of the 20th century. At the end of the century, his granddaughter Flavie Revillon and Agathe Letellier, Flavie's daughter, decided to specialize in the production of cider, Pommeau de Normandie, and Calvados. The estate consists of a beautiful manor surrounded by 25 hectares of traditional high-stem apples trees at Pennedepie near Honfleur. The orchard includes 17 apple varieties, and was reconverted into organic production in 2012.

Calvados Adrien Camut

For seven generations, the Camut family has been producing Calvados at Domaine de Sémainville in Lalande Saint Léger. The Domaine consists of 45 hectares of high-stem apple trees, and is allowed Pays d'Auge appellation status.

Adrien Camut (1908-1989) was one of the region's legendary producers who made the family name famous. He was an innovator, creating a unique wood-burning pot still of sophisticated design that is still used today. His son Claude succeeded him in 1989 and retired in 2002. Claude had three sons, Jean Michel, Emmanuel, and Jean-Gabriel who took over. Calvados is aged mostly in large old oak barrels.

Calvados Le Père Jules

This agricultural producer was founded in 1919 at Saint Désir de Lisieux. Léon Desfrieches, son to the founder Jules, launched the brand "Le Père Jules" as a tribute to his father after joining the estate in 1949. The fruits come from 43 hectares of high stem apple trees. Today, Léon's son Thierry Desfrieches and his son Guillaume, , an oenologist, run the estate. The eldest son, Hughes, bought another farm in Sainte-Marguerite-de-Carrouges in the Orne district. On the opposite side of the road Valery Desfrieches, a son of Léon Desfrieches, runs the only cooperage left in Calvados.

Domaine de la Galotière

In 1963, Claude Olivier bought the estate, which is now managed by his son Jean-Luc Olivier and Pascal Choisnars, Jean-Luc's brother-in-law. The farm is located in Crouttes, 10 kilometers from Sainte-Foy-de-Montgommery. They have both types of orchards on the property: high-stem and low-stem. In 2004 they bought a pot still to produce Calvados Pays d'Auge. Calvados is aged in well-seasoned barrels. The production is now certified organic.

Calvados Giard

The Giard family produces Calvados Pays d'Auge at Domaine du Manoir de Montreuil at Grandouet near Cambremer in Pays d'Auge. The Giard history on the estate can be traced back to the 1700s. Today, they grow 30 hectares of traditional high-stem apple trees, produce cider with a modern press, distill it in a 15hl pot still, and age Calvados in old oak casks. Michèle and Patrice Giard and their daughter Estelle run the production

Calvados du Lieu Chéri

Serge Desfrièches, a cousin of Leon Desfrièches, started producing Calvados Pays d'Auge in 1946 in a 16th century estate at Ouilly Le Vicomte. Serge's son, Fabrice, took over in 1997. In 2005 his son Alexandre joined the family business. Fruits come from both high and low stem apple trees. They are pressed and distilled on the farm. The Calvados is aged in oak barrels from various origins.

▶ Domfrontais Farmer-Producers

Calvados Comte Louis de Lauriston

Located in Domfront in the Orne district, the Chais du Verger Normand, in collaboration with the Drouin family, is the major actor in the Appellation Domfrontais.

Founded by Count Louis de Lauriston in 1962 to put an end to the illicit distilling of Calvados in the Domfrontais region, les Chais du Verger Normand ages and bottles Calvados produced by farmers in Domfrontais.

In 1992, Christian Drouin became a partner and began marketing their products. Since 2008, Guillaume Drouin has managed the cooperative as President. Most of the distillation is done on the producer's estate by Daniel Guesdon's mobile still. On average, the Calvados is made from 60% pears and 40% apples. The freshly distilled spirit is transported to les Chais du Verger Normand, where it ages in old oak casks. The brand Comte Louis de Lauriston offers a unique range of vintages dating back to the period of clandestine production. Les chais du Verger Normand also sells Calvados under the Guillaume de Normandie brand.

Calvados Didier Lemorton

Isidore Lemorton, a legendary producer in Domfrontais, was born in 1900 and made the name famous. I will always remember my meeting with Isidore Lemorton, one of the greatest characters of Calvados, who had expressed desire to see me when I published, along with Jacques Billy, *Le Grand Livre des Calvados*. Far back in the Norman bocage, he welcomed me into his office. Behind him I could see a rack with an impressive number of rifles, most likely meant to discourage pestersome intruders. In spite of his age he was a splendid man. He offered me an unforgettable tasting of his oldest Calvados, which had kept amazing freshness.

When he died in 1994, his five children — two sons, Louis and Roger, and three daughters — inherited a share of the stock. Roger Lemorton inherited the property, la Baillée Fêtu in Mantilly. The farm comprises some 100 hectares. The orchard consists of high-stem pear and apple trees. Roger's son Didier moved into Isidore's house and Roger moved into a bordering property. Didier now runs the domaine, using 70% of pears. Other Domfrontais names such as Pacory, Guesdon, Victor Gontier, and Domaine de la Duretière might be difficult to find in the United States.

▶ Calvados Farmer-Producers

Claque Pépin

Claque Pépin, named after an apple variety, is run by Benoit Louvet, an agricultural producer and independent bottler at Serans near Argentan in the Orne. The premises are located next to Château de Serans, which his grandfather had bought in the early 1900s and that his father sold at the end of the 1990s, retaining some land and farm buildings now used to store cider, perry cider, and Calvados. Benoit Louvet is a born entrepreneur. He came and met me at the end of the 1990s to explore the possibility of collaborating on a perry project. Unfortunately, it was not the best timing for me to start another project. He started his business in 2003, and is now emerging as a significant player.

▶ Negoçiants and Independent Bottlers

A negoçiant or an independent bottler buys Calvados that he bottles directly, or after additional aging and blending at his facilities. For many years, only a few producers were keen on exporting on distant markets. This vacuum was noticed by some Cognac houses which use their international distribution network to sell other products including Calvados which is bought bottled or in bulk from Calvados distilleries.

Calvados Lelouvier and Guillaume de Normandie

André Lelouvier started his business as a wine and spirit merchant in 1933 in Briouze in the Orne area. He bought Calvados from carefully selected small growers in La Ferté Macé and Domfront areas, and began to age them at la Ferté Macé in the Domaine des Champs, André Lelouvier's home. Calvados was marketed under Lelouvier and Guillaume de Normandie brand names.

In the seventies he founded Calvados Lelouvier so that he could hand down the company to his 11 children. His son Christian took over the management. Christian Lelouvier was a jolly man who loved eating in good restaurants that happened to be his customers, such as Le Central in Trouville. We soon became friends and I enjoyed having lunch with him. Although none of his children were interested in taking the business over, he would have liked Calvados Lelouvier's adventure to go on, as he told me on several occasions. He hoped I might be interested. In 2016, on Christian Lelouvier's death, the business was taken over by Calvados Christian Drouin SAS. The company still works with the same farmers.

30&40

30/40 is an independent bottler created in 2015. They actively promote an aperitif called "Double Jus" designed for mixing.

Calvados Daron

Daron is a brand of Calvados Pays d'Auge marketed by a French company, Maison Ferrand, specializing in the production and marketing of fine spirits with a focus on Cognac (Pierre Ferrand), rum and gin.

Calvados Menorval

Menorval is a Calvados brand marketed by the Prunier Cognac firm.

Père Francois

Père Francois is a brand marketed by Gautier Cognac.

Most likely some producers exporting to the US may not appear in this list compiled with the available information.

Epilogue

Every year many Americans and Canadians take advantage of a trip to Normandy to visit Calvados producers. I invite those who have not yet come to do so. It's one of the best ways to discover one of the most beautiful regions of France.

Domaine Christian Drouin, Pont-l'Evêque

Bibliography

Calvados books published in English:

Calvados, The Spirit of Normandy. Charles Neal. Flame Grape Press, San Francisco, USA, 2011.

The World's Premier Apple Brandy. Henrik Mattsson, Sweden, 2004.

From the same author:

Le Livre Des Calvados, Des Racines Normandes, Une Ambition Mondiale. Christian Drouin, Preface by Nicole Ameline. Editions Charles Corlet, France, 2020. *Grand Prix du Livre Spirit 2020*

Calvados Book (in Japanese). Christian Drouin, Preface by Hiroyuki Takayama. Taru Publishing Company, Japan, 2020.

Petit Guide au Coeur de la Cuisine Normande. Béatrice and Christian Drouin. Éditions Charles Corlet, France, 2013.

Les Cocktails Normands, Guide de 77 Recettes. Jean-Paul Thomine and Christian Drouin. Éditions Charles Corlet, France, 2009.

Les Cocktails Normands, Guide de 138 Recettes. Jean-Paul Thomine and Christian Drouin. Éditions Charles Corlet, France, 2006.

Normandy Cocktails, A Guide For 138 Recipes. Jean-Paul Thomine and Christian Drouin, Éditions Charles Corlet, France, 2005.

Au Coeur de la Cuisine Normande, 101 Recettes. Béatrice and Christian Drouin, Preface by Pierre Androuet. Éditions Charles Corlet, France, 2001.

Guide des Cocktails à Base de Cognac, 121 Recettes. Jean-Paul Thomine and Christian Drouin. Éditions Charles Corlet, France, 2000.

Guide des Cocktails à Base de Calvados, 121 Recettes. Jean-Paul Thomine and Christian Drouin. Éditions Charles Corlet, France, 1999.

Pommeau de Normandie. Christian Drouin, preface by Jacques Puisais. Éditions Charles Corlet, France, 1991. *Prix de l'Académie Normande.*

Cocktails en Normandie. Jean-Paul Thomine and Christian Drouin, preface by David de Rothschild. Éditions Charles Corlet, France, 1988. English edition: *Cocktails from Normandy*, 1988. German edition: *Cocktails aus der Normandie*, 1990.

Le Grand Livre des Calvados. Jacques Billy and Christian Drouin, preface by Jean Pinchon. Éditions Charles Corlet, France, 1987. *Prix de l'ordre mondial des gourmets dégustateurs.*

Découverte des Liqueurs et Eaux-de-vie. Christian Drouin, Editions La Presse-Le collège Marie-Victorin, Montréal, Canada, 1982.

Acknowledgments

This book has been quite a long time in the making. I don't think it would have been materialized at all without the numerous requests received from all over the world to find out if a version of my book" Le Livre des Calvados" was available in English. After the almost simultaneous publication of a version in Japanese, I hoped to be able to release a version intended for the American market, but finding a publisher ready to take on the challenge of publishing a book on a niche product required a lot of motivation, and Covid made the situation even more complicated.

I wish to express my gratitude to spirits authorities convinced that Calvados was one of the greatest brandies deserving better recognition, who always supported me in my work of evangelization, particularly Paul Pacult, Sean Ludford, Flavien Desoblin of Brandy Library and those who sadly left us, Anthony Dias Blue, Gary Regan, and Michael Jackson. I particularly want to thank Jason Wilson who encouraged me, helped me to improve the cocktail section, and wrote the preface. I would like to warmly thank Eric Gaudet, creator of first Spirit Salon in France, who helped me find a publisher by organizing a meeting in Paris with Bill Owens. Thanks to Margarett Waterbury, the editor, who improved significantly the manuscript and Gail Sands, the book designer. Thanks to IDAC for the information and photos given. My debt to my wife Béatrice at every stage in the preparation of the "Art of Calvados."

WHITE MULE PRESS

www.ingramcontent.com/pod-product-compliance
Lightning Source LLC
Chambersburg PA
CBHW041239240426
43661CB00071B/2921